Fun, Quick & Easy

Game-Based Activities for Teachers of Adult ESL

Written & Illustrated by
Gisele L. White

Dedicated to my fellow ESL teachers who have supported, shared, and commiserated with me. This book is my "Thank you."

A very special thanks to Mom and Jack for your help and encouragement. Who knew writing a book was so much... WORK!?

* This cartoon is for comic effect only.
No sheets of paper were harmed during the computer drafting of this book.
Please share the use of this book with your friends and fellow teachers.
Reduce, Reuse, Recycle.

Text, illustrations & cover art copyright (c) 2008 by Gisele L. White. All rights reserved.

The Professor Melonhead logo is a registered trademark.

ISBN 978-0-615-24840-0

Table of Contents

INTRODUCTION	6
CHAPTER 1.	9
The Interview	
Giving & receiving basic personal information	
CHAPTER 2.	17
Alphabet Hot Potato	
Learning the alphabet	
CHAPTER 3.	21
1-2-3 Write!	
Saying, hearing & writing numbers	
CHAPTER 4.	49
ZINGO!	
Listening comprehension with numbers	
CHAPTER 5.	71
Exact Change	
Listening comprehension with U.S. currency	
CHAPTER 6.	79
Map of the United States	
U.S. geography & state abbreviations	
CHAPTER 7.	85
May I Ask Who's Calling?	
Leaving & taking basic phone messages	

Table of Contents

CHAPTER 8.	95
Architect	
Prepositions of place	
CHAPTER 9.	107
Preposition Bluff	
Advanced lesson in prepositions	
CHAPTER 10.	115
Guess My Occupation	
Asking & answering questions about occupations	
CHAPTER 11.	121
Name That Shop	
Vocabulary building for places of business	
CHAPTER 12.	131
Where's the Post Office?	
Giving & receiving directions	
CHAPTER 13.	147
Hangman for Small Talk	
Reinforcing small talk skills	
CHAPTER 14.	151
Drawn to Homonyms	
Vocabulary building with homonyms	

Table of Contents

CHAPTER 15.   157
Present Perfect Speed
    Conjugating present perfect irregular verbs

CHAPTER 16.   163
Grocery Shopping
    Vocabulary building for food & shopping

CHAPTER 17.   175
What's Cooking?
    Explaining a process

CHAPTER 18.   181
Talking Trivia
    Developing speaking & listening skills through trivia

CHAPTER 19.   193
Whisper
    Pre-test review for large classes

CHAPTER 20.   197
You Must Be Joking
    Developing speaking & listening skills through joke telling

APPENDIX   209

Introduction

The focus of my ESL career has been the on-site teaching of Business English to company employees overseas. This book is designed with such a teacher in mind.

I've found that putting the learning process in the hands of the students as much as possible works best. Here you will find a variety of pre-tested, game-oriented lesson plans that you can either photocopy directly from this book or use as inspiration or guidance for designing your own unique lesson plans. These lessons are designed to take the focus off of you, The Teacher, and disperse it throughout the class so that your students are actively interacting with and learning from each other rather than passively staring at you for two hours.

The purpose of this book is to provide supplementary lesson plans that breathe life into the English language and approach the learning process from a more relaxed, game-oriented perspective. Many of these lessons involve partner work or students working in small groups. The teacher's role with most of these lessons is to supervise, correct, and answer any questions that may crop up.

Nothing in this book is the definitive way to do anything. The lesson preparation descriptions are what have worked for me in the past, but you are, of course, free to alter these plans as you see fit. Furthermore, there is no reason why you can't, within reason, use these lessons for classes of varying levels. It's just a matter of how long it takes for each class to get through each lesson. Most of these lesson plans are for classes of 3 to 15 students. This book is not designed for private one-on-one tutors.

Introduction

This book is for the nervous teacher facing his/her first class as well as the brain-fried veteran trying to come up with fresh ideas. You may find that there is more material offered here than you could possibly need for a single lesson. An abundance of choices is provided so that you can custom-tailor the lesson to each class's specific needs and levels of proficiency, thus avoiding the "one size fits all" approach to lesson planning.

With *Fun, Quick & Easy: Game-Based Activities for Teachers of Adult ESL*, you need spend only 5-10 minutes preparing for each lesson. If you find a lesson that you particularly like and plan to use over again, consider ways to laminate the cards, sheets, game boards, etc. and collect them after every lesson, thus further reducing your prep time. Or place cut-outs in clearly labeled envelopes that you can easily grab just before you head out the door for future classes.

The activities that I designed and compiled in this book helped me teach the English language to non-native speakers, both in the United States and abroad, in an entertaining and engaging manner. I hope this book helps you to find success in your ESL career as well.

Chapter 1. **The Interview** Directions

OBJECTIVE:

To set a precedent of students interacting with each other and getting to know their fellow classmates.

HOW TO PREPARE FOR THIS LESSON:

Photocopy enough of the **The Interview** Activity Sheet for each student and yourself.

Divide the class into partners. If you have an odd number of students, make one group of three students: Student A will interview Student B, Student B will interview Student C, and Student C will interview Student A.

Go over the vocabulary on the sheet as a class to make sure everyone understands words like "nationality" and terms like "marital status."

Then make sure they can ask basic questions for each item on the sheet.

NOW BEGIN:

After you have gone through each item, have the students interview their partner and write down their partner's information on the list. Your job at this point is to go around and make sure they are speaking only in English and to correct any errors in grammar, pronunciation, etc. and to answer any

Page 9

Business Relevance

This is a relatively non-threatening way to get students used to public speaking in English.

Having students ask random questions at the end of the lesson helps the speaker learn to field questions and to literally think on their feet.

Save A Tree
Save Some Time

Cover both sides of **The Interview** Sample Questions with clear packing tape before cutting them into strips. This will make them more durable for repeated use.

Collect the strips at the end of each lesson and place them in a labeled envelope for future use.

Chapter 1. The Interview   Directions

A Bright Idea!

Try to use the time you spend going over the vocabulary and questions to gauge each student's level of language proficiency. If possible, try to pair the more advanced students with the struggling students because:

- A more advanced partnership will finish faster than a struggling partnership. If the advanced student has to slow down to explain things to his/her partner, there's a better chance that the whole class will finish the lesson around the same time.

- You can use the more advanced students to help you in class. It's a good confidence booster for them to be able to help their partner and keeps them actively participating even if the lesson is a tad below their level.

questions they may have.

When the interviewing is over, have one pair of students go to the front of the class. Have one half of the partnership introduce the other to the class. Then vice versa. Choose a seated student to ask a new question of either of the students at the front of the class. Then move on to the next pair. Again, your role is to correct any errors that may arise in grammar, syntax, pronunciation, etc.

VARIATION:

To review this lesson during the following class, put a pile of question strips in the middle of the table, face down, and have each student pick one question from the pile at random to ask another student. Four sheets of **The Interview** Sample Questions are provided at the end of this chapter.

Try to prompt the less forthcoming students to speak more when the opportunity presents itself. If someone asks them if they have any kids, they can offer more than simply "Yes." For example, "I have one son and two daughters." The student asking the question should also feel free to ask follow-up questions. For example, "How old are your kids?" or "I also have kids—one son and one daughter."

The Interview Activity Sheet

Name	
Age	
Birth Date	
Nationality	
Language(s)	
Marital Status	
Children (age)	
Siblings	
Pets	
Birthplace	
Occupation	
Company Name	
Do you like your job? (Why? / Why not?)	
Favorite Food(s)	
Favorite TV Show(s)	
Favorite Vacation Destination(s) (Why?)	
Hobbies	

Chapter 1. **The Interview** Sample Questions #1

What is your name?

What is your first name?

What is your last name?

Can you spell your first name (please)?

How do you spell your last name?

How old are you?

What is your birth date?

When were you born?

Where were you born?

Where are you from?

What's your nationality?

Are you married?

What is your marital status?

How long have you been married?

Do you have any children?

Chapter 1. **The Interview** Sample Questions #2

How many children do you have?

How old are your children?

Do you have any pets?

Do you have any brothers or sisters?

Do you have any siblings?

What is your favorite TV show?

Have you read any good books lately?

Have you seen any good movies lately?

Have you been to any good restaurants lately?

What are your hobbies?

What do you like to do in your free time?

What kind of music do you like?

Do you like sports?

Are you a good cook?

Can you sing?

Chapter 1. **The Interview**   Sample Questions #3

What place would you like to visit?

Are you athletic?

Are you artistic?

Are you musical?

Do you like to paint?

How many languages do you speak?

What do you do for a living?

What is your job?

Who do you work for?

What company do you work for?

How long have you worked for your company?

Do you like your job?

What is your favorite color?

What is your favorite food?

What is your favorite vacation destination?

Chapter 1. **The Interview** Sample Questions #4

What kind of movies do you like?

Do you prefer coffee or tea?

Do you prefer indoor activities or outdoor activities?

What's your favorite season?

What is one thing you'd like to do before you die?

Can you play a musical instrument?

What's your favorite holiday?

What did you do for your last vacation?

Do you prefer wine or beer?

What famous person would you like to meet?

Are you a spender or a saver?

Are you a morning person or a night owl?

Are you an optimist or a pessimist?

Are you an introvert or an extrovert?

Are you a liberal or a conservative?

Chapter 2. Alphabet Hot Potato — Directions

OBJECTIVE:

For absolute beginners to learn the alphabet.

You may find that your more advanced students still struggle with certain letters so it might be fun to try a few rounds with them as well.

HOW TO PREPARE FOR THIS LESSON:

Depending on your class size, bring one or more balls to class. It would be best to use softer balls that aren't likely to cause bodily injury; for example, tennis balls, nerf balls, or hacky sacks.

Write the alphabet on the board in big letters and go over it in class. When you feel they have learned it pretty well, divide the class, if necessary, into groups of 4-6 students. Clear some space on the floor so each group can spread out and make a circle. Give each group a ball, a.k.a. a "hot potato."

NOW BEGIN:

Explain that the ball is actually a hot potato, and therefore they cannot hold it for a long time. Toss the potato (ball) to one student and say "A". Point to the receiving student and say "B", indicating that he/she should say "B". Gesture for the ball to be tossed back to you and say "C". Toss it to another

Caution !

Baseballs, softballs, volleyballs or soccer balls can cause serious bodily injury and are not recommended for this lesson.

Large beach balls are fun, since they are light, colorful, and easy to catch due to their size. However, they are hard to fit into a briefcase.

Chapter 2. **Alphabet Hot Potato**   Directions

Page 18

Caution !

Clear desks and chairs out of the way as much as possible before you begin this lesson.

Check the floor for stray pens, pencils, or pieces of chalk —anything that might cause someone to slip or trip.

student who should then say "D", and so on. Step out of the group and let the students toss the ball to each other and go through the alphabet on their own.

They need to work as a group to try to get through the entire alphabet perfectly, without hesitation, and without dropping the hot potato. If one of the students drops the ball, hesitates, or can't come up with the next letter of the alphabet, they have to start from the beginning.

When the class is able to get through a few rounds perfectly, erase the alphabet from the board and see how they do. If they can still get through the entire alphabet, rewrite the alphabet on the board in big letters. Have the students call out the letters you point to at random. Can they easily recall individual letters when they're not in A to Z order? Have different students go to the board and randomly choose letters for their classmates to call out. Try both upper and lower case letters, if you have time.

VARIATIONS:

You can also use the Hot Potato game for other skills. If the alphabet is too easy, try having your students say words that begin with each letter of the alphabet. For example, "A – Apple", then "B – Bat", "C – Carrot", and so on. Or numbers from zero

Chapter 2. Alphabet Hot Potato — Directions

to one hundred. This game can be used for basic small talk questions and answers. For example, "What is your name?"; "My name is John."; "Where are you from?"; "I'm from Spain."

Your role during this game is basically to keep it honest. If someone makes a mistake, make sure their group starts from the beginning and that they aren't just blundering through it.

Hot Potato can be used for an entire lesson to review various skills learned in previous lessons, or it can be used more sparingly as a supplement to that day's lesson. Either way, your students will probably appreciate the opportunity to get out of their seats and move around a bit. My students always did.

For interactive, on-line activities, try:

- ProfessorMelonhead.com/Alphabet_UpperCase.html
- ProfessorMelonhead.com/Alphabet_LowerCase.html

A Bright Idea !

If the weather is nice, try taking this lesson outside.

Some companies have nice, spacious green areas. However, if the best you can manage is the company parking lot, I would just stay in the classroom.

Chapter 3. 1-2-3 Write! Directions

OBJECTIVE:

To get students comfortable saying and hearing numbers clearly.

HOW TO PREPARE FOR THIS LESSON:

Photocopy enough **1-2-3 Write!** Study Sheets for each student and yourself.

Photocopy some **1-2-3 Write!** Game Chips. You'll find that there are several sheets of numbers, ranging from low to high numbers. Choose a subsection that best fits your class's level.

PRONUNCIATION:

Make clear the difference in stress on the first syllable of numbers *twen*ty, *thir*ty, *for*ty, *fif*ty, *six*ty, *seven*ty, *eigh*ty, and *nine*ty, as opposed to the stress on the second syllable for numbers thir*teen*, four*teen*, fif*teen*, six*teen*, seven*teen*, eigh*teen,* and nine*teen*.

NOW BEGIN:

Divide the class into two teams. Two players from the same team go to the front of the class.

Player A is the Reader and Player B is the Writer. Remind the class prior to each round that the

---

A Good Precursor to:

- May I Ask Who's Calling?
- ZINGO!
- Exact Change
- Grocery Shopping

**Save A Tree
Save Some Time**

Cover both sides of **1-2-3 Write!** Game Chips with clear packing tape before cutting them into individual chips. This will make them more durable for repeated use.

Collect the chips at the end of each lesson and place them in a labeled envelope for future use.

Chapter 3. **1-2-3 Write!**   Directions

Save A Tree

If you do not have the use of a whiteboard or chalkboard and don't want to buy writing paper, just have Player B (The Writer) write at the table using recycled office paper. The bins by the photocopy machines are usually full of discarded paper.

As long as the paper is not crumpled and one side is blank, this should work fine.

numbers must be written clearly. If Player B writes too fast and the numbers are illegible, their team cannot earn points for those numbers.

Player A picks up a game chip, reads the number aloud, and then sets it aside in a separate pile. Player B writes the number down.

The objective is to get through as many numbers as they can, within a certain period of time (30-45 seconds is good) to earn points—one point for each number written correctly.

When the time is up, go through each number that Player A has set aside and compare it with the numbers that Player B has written. For each number that is written correctly, their team earns a point.

Mix the used game chips back in with the rest of the numbers and continue playing. Two players from the opposing team then go to the front and start a new round.

It's best to use a chalkboard/whiteboard, if possible, so that the other students have the option of simultaneously writing at their seats and checking their work as well. If you do not have access to a whiteboard or chalkboard, bring a stack of paper for the students to write their numbers on.

Chapter 3. **1-2-3 Write!**   Directions

Page 23

VARIATIONS:

Focusing on game chips to tell time (page 40) would be a good transition to the **Time-O!** lesson (page 211).

Focusing on game chips for U.S. currency (page 46) would be a good transition to the **Exact Change** lesson (page 71).

To transition into the **May I Ask Who's Calling?** lesson (page 85), try using the **Phone Number Speed** Game Chips located in the Appendix (page 245).

For an interactive, on-line activity, try:

○ ProfessorMelonhead.com/Spelling_Numbers.html

Cheater Alert !

When the number is two digits or longer, some of your students may try to say the number broken down by single digits.

For example, rather than saying "one hundred and twenty-three," they might try to get a bit sneaky and say "one, two, three" instead.

Make it clear at the start of this lesson that no points will be awarded unless the numbers are said properly.

* However, in the case of **Phone Number Speed**, the students should say each individual number.

1-2-3 Write! Study Sheet

0	zero				
1	one			100	one hundred
2	two			200	two hundred
3	three	30	thirty	300	three hundred
4	four	40	forty	400	four hundred
5	five	50	fifty	500	five hundred
6	six	60	sixty	600	six hundred
7	seven	70	seventy	700	seven hundred
8	eight	80	eighty	800	eight hundred
9	nine	90	ninety	900	nine hundred
10	ten				
11	eleven				
12	twelve				
13	thirteen				
14	fourteen				
15	fifteen				
16	sixteen				
17	seventeen				
18	eighteen				
19	nineteen				

1,000	one thousand
10,000	ten thousand
100,000	one hundred thousand
1,000,000	one million
10,000,000	ten million
100,000,000	one hundred million
1,000,000,000	one billion

20	twenty
21	twenty-one
22	twenty-two
23	twenty-three
24	twenty-four
25	twenty-five
26	twenty-six
27	twenty-seven
28	twenty-eight
29	twenty-nine

Currency

.50	fifty cents
$1.25	one dollar and twenty-five cents
$21.01	twenty-one dollars and one cent

Time of Day

12:05	twelve o' five
11:02	eleven o' two
10:10	ten ten
9:30	nine thirty
8:45	eight forty-five

Chapter 3.   **1-2-3 Write!**   Game Chips #1

1	2	3
4	5	6
7	8	9
10	11	12
13	14	15
16	17	18
19	20	21
22	23	24
25	26	27
28	29	30

31	32	33
34	35	36
37	38	39
40	41	42
43	44	45
46	47	48
49	50	51
52	53	54
55	56	57
58	59	60

Chapter 3.   1-2-3 Write!   Game Chips #3

61	62	63
64	65	66
67	68	69
70	71	72
73	74	75
76	77	78
79	80	81
82	83	84
85	86	87
88	89	90

91	92	93
94	95	96
97	98	99
100	200	300
400	500	600
700	800	900
101	108	110
123	125	137
148	142	150
155	181	199

Chapter 3.   1-2-3 Write!   Game Chips #5

202	205	209
211	212	216
227	239	240
250	254	261
273	280	295
301	303	306
313	316	317
326	333	339
346	351	365
374	388	392

401	408	409
414	418	411
428	436	447
444	451	469
476	482	499
502	507	508
511	516	517
524	537	545
555	564	579
571	583	590

Chapter 3. **1-2-3 Write!** Game Chips #7

601	603	606
613	617	619
624	632	645
658	660	676
681	695	699
702	703	706
711	714	716
728	737	740
750	756	766
777	783	790

 Chapter 3. **1-2-3 Write!** Game Chips #8

802	804	807
812	815	818
820	834	840
847	856	868
871	880	893
902	905	909
911	916	918
926	938	947
956	960	977
986	991	999

Chapter 3. 1-2-3 Write! Game Chips #9

1,000	2,000	3,000
4,000	5,000	6,000
7,000	8,000	9,000
10,000	11,000	12,000
13,000	14,000	15,000
16,000	17,000	18,000
19,000	20,000	30,000
40,000	50,000	60,000
70,000	80,000	90,000
25,000	35,000	45,000

55,000	65,000	75,000
85,000	95,000	22,000
33,000	44,000	55,000
66,000	77,000	88,000
99,000	21,000	31,000
41,000	51,000	61,000
71,000	81,000	91,000
23,000	32,000	42,000
52,000	62,000	72,000
82,000	92,000	43,000

Chapter 3.   **1-2-3 Write!**   Game Chips #11

46,000	53,000	63,000
73,000	83,000	93,000
24,000	34,000	54,000
64,000	74,000	84,000
94,000	26,000	36,000
47,000	56,000	67,000
76,000	86,000	96,000
27,000	37,000	47,000
57,000	67,000	78,000
89,000	97,000	28,000

38,000	48,000	58,000
68,000	78,000	98,000
29,000	39,000	49,000
59,000	69,000	79,000
89,000	1,111	2,222
3,333	4,444	5,555
6,666	7,777	8,888
9,999	1,001	2,002
3,003	4,004	5,005
6,006	7,007	8,008

Chapter 3. **1-2-3 Write!** Game Chips #13

1,459	2,658	3,615
4,305	5,747	6,914
7,379	8,234	9,556
10,511	11,487	12,613
13,794	14,509	15,937
16,054	17,817	18,326
19,231	20,901	30,750
40,863	50,139	60,289
70,356	80,471	90,562
81,568	49,804	24,780

1,284	2,902	3,654
4,813	5,019	6,461
7,547	8,931	9,077
10,637	11,991	12,462
13,225	14,081	15,662
16,483	17,726	18,643
19,354	26,107	38,618
45,282	57,641	62,823
73,294	81,555	94,317
29,125	36,048	42,561

53,601	67,233	78,488
112,928	149,911	111,936
293,293	213,879	245,009
397,026	391,485	340,671
402,723	463,002	444,717
527,994	515,550	531,312
602,784	615,111	660,616
719,091	712,005	785,313
863,913	809,413	880,618
909,201	997,882	919,290

12:00 a.m.	12:05 a.m.	12:10 a.m.
12:15 p.m.	12:20 p.m.	12:25 p.m.
12:30 a.m.	12:35 a.m.	12:40 a.m.
12:45 p.m.	12:50 p.m.	12:55 p.m.
1:00 p.m.	1:05 p.m.	1:10 p.m.
1:15 a.m.	1:20 a.m.	1:25 a.m.
1:30 p.m.	1:35 p.m.	1:40 p.m.
1:45 a.m.	1:50 a.m.	1:55 a.m.
2:00 a.m.	2:05 a.m.	2:10 a.m.
2:15 p.m.	2:20 p.m.	2:25 p.m.

2:30 a.m.	2:35 a.m.	2:40 a.m.
2:45 p.m.	2:50 p.m.	2:55 p.m.
3:00 a.m.	3:05 a.m.	3:10 a.m.
3:15 p.m.	3:20 p.m.	3:25 p.m.
3:30 p.m.	3:35 p.m.	3:40 p.m.
3:45 a.m.	3:50 a.m.	3:55 a.m.
4:00 p.m.	4:05 p.m.	4:10 p.m.
4:15 a.m.	4:20 a.m.	4:25 a.m.
4:30 a.m.	4:35 a.m.	4:40 a.m.
4:45 p.m.	4:50 p.m.	4:55 p.m.

5:00 a.m.	5:05 a.m.	5:10 a.m.
5:15 p.m.	5:20 p.m.	5:25 p.m.
5:30 a.m.	5:35 a.m.	5:40 a.m.
5:45 p.m.	5:50 p.m.	5:55 p.m.
6:00 p.m.	6:05 p.m.	6:10 p.m.
6:15 a.m.	6:20 a.m.	6:25 a.m.
6:30 p.m.	6:35 p.m.	6:40 p.m.
6:45 a.m.	6:50 a.m.	6:55 a.m.
7:00 a.m.	7:05 a.m.	7:10 a.m.
7:15 p.m.	7:20 p.m.	7:25 p.m.

7:30 a.m.	7:35 a.m.	7:40 a.m.
7:45 p.m.	7:50 p.m.	7:55 p.m.
8:00 a.m.	8:05 a.m.	8:10 a.m.
8:15 p.m.	8:20 p.m.	8:25 p.m.
8:30 p.m.	8:35 p.m.	8:40 p.m.
8:45 a.m.	8:50 a.m.	8:55 a.m.
9:00 p.m.	9:05 p.m.	9:10 p.m.
9:15 a.m.	9:20 a.m.	9:25 a.m.
9:30 a.m.	9:35 a.m.	9:40 a.m.
9:45 p.m.	9:50 p.m.	9:55 p.m.

10:00 a.m.	10:05 a.m.	10:10 a.m.
10:15 p.m.	10:20 p.m.	10:25 p.m.
10:30 a.m.	10:35 a.m.	10:40 a.m.
10:45 p.m.	10:50 p.m.	10:55 p.m.
11:00 p.m.	11:05 p.m.	11:10 p.m.
11:15 a.m.	11:20 a.m.	11:25 a.m.
11:30 p.m.	11:35 p.m.	11:40 p.m.
11:45 a.m.	11:50 a.m.	11:55 a.m.
1:06 a.m.	2:12 a.m.	3:27 a.m.
4:38 p.m.	5:41 p.m.	6:53 p.m.

Chapter 3. **1-2-3 Write!** Game Chips Time #6

7:02 a.m.	8:17 a.m.	9:23 a.m.
10:34 p.m.	11:48 p.m.	12:59 p.m.
1:52 a.m.	2:46 a.m.	3:36 a.m.
4:28 p.m.	5:13 p.m.	6:04 p.m.
7:08 p.m.	8:57 p.m.	9:49 p.m.
10:11 a.m.	11:22 a.m.	12:26 a.m.
1:38 p.m.	2:39 p.m.	3:42 p.m.
4:42 a.m.	5:51 a.m.	6:57 a.m.
7:16 a.m.	8:12 a.m.	9:27 a.m.
10:18 p.m.	11:37 p.m.	12:54 p.m.

$1.25	$2.45	$3.56
$4.77	$5.92	$6.53
$7.89	$8.13	$9.03
$10.23	$11.41	$12.36
$13.59	$14.71	$15.33
$16.74	$17.18	$18.07
$19.55	$20.21	$21.72
$22.63	$23.48	$24.86
$25.31	$26.11	$27.09
$28.52	$29.76	$30.22

$31.64	$32.99	$33.42
$34.52	$35.54	$36.65
$37.79	$38.29	$39.35
$40.98	$41.31	$42.30
$43.32	$44.14	$45.63
$46.95	$47.17	$48.35
$49.47	$50.81	$51.70
$52.57	$53.12	$54.27
$55.36	$56.84	$57.68
$58.13	$59.13	$60.90

$61.25	$62.67	$63.24
$64.46	$65.97	$66.24
$67.43	$68.46	$69.56
$70.88	$71.38	$72.24
$73.79	$74.23	$75.04
$76.41	$77.23	$78.72
$79.86	$80.26	$81.44
$82.56	$83.92	$84.89
$85.66	$86.31	$87.36
$88.45	$89.93	$90.77

Chapter 4. ZINGO! Directions

OBJECTIVE:

For beginner level classes to perfect their ability to say and hear numbers and letters clearly or as a warm-up or review for more advanced students.

HOW TO PREPARE FOR THIS LESSON:

This game is basically a variation on Bingo, with which you already may be familiar..

Photocopy enough **ZINGO!** Game Sheets for each student. Photocopy and cut the **ZINGO!** Game Chips into their individual pieces.

If you have a smaller class of 4-5 students, then just photocopy 6-7 game sheets. Students sometimes like the option of exchanging their current game sheet for one that is "luckier." Fifteen game sheets are included for larger conversation classes.

You will also need place markers so the students can cover the squares on their game sheet when they are called out. You can get as fancy with this as you like but recycled office paper cut into squares has always worked well for me.

NOW BEGIN:

When you are ready to start this lesson, put the **ZINGO!** Game Chips, face down, at the head of the table. Ask one student, Student A, to join you

A Good Precursor to:

- May I Ask Who's Calling?

- Exact Change

- Grocery Shopping

Chapter 4. ZINGO! Directions

Page 50

Save A Tree

You can use discarded paper from the paper recycling bins to make **ZINGO!** place markers.

You can either cut the sheets into nice little squares or, if you're feeling lazy, hand a sheet to each student and they can tear off bits of paper as they play.

at the head of the table.

Have the other students choose their own **ZINGO!** Game Sheet.

Explain that each game chip has a letter/number combination on it. Show one to the class. Student A will choose a game chip at random and say the letter/number combination on it. Student A does not show the game chip to the rest of the class. The rest of the students have to try to find the same letter/number combination on their game sheet that matches the one that has been said. If they find a match, they are to put a place marker over the box that contains that particular combination. Student A saves that game chip to the side, chooses a new game chip, reads the letter/number combination, and so on.

The first student to cover five boxes in a row—horizontally, vertically, or diagonally—yells "ZINGO!" Student A must then confirm that they have covered the correct squares by going through the pile of chips that were set to the side.

If the correct squares have been covered, the player must read all five letter/number combinations to show that he/she really knows what they are and didn't just get lucky. If all is

Chapter 4. **ZINGO!** Directions

satisfactory, the player is declared the winner and takes his/her place at the head of the table to begin a new game as the new Student A. If not, the student goes back to his/her seat and the game continues until there's a winner.

After a winner is declared, the used game chips are mixed back in with the main pile. Student A returns to his/her seat and selects a game sheet and the winner goes to the head of the table and begins choosing game chips and calling them out for the next round.

Your role is to simply watch over Student A's shoulder to make sure that he/she is calling out the letter/number combinations correctly and with clear pronunciation.

Variation:

To use this same format to help students say and hear the time of day, **Time-O!** Game Chips, **Time-O!** Game Sheets, and a **Time-O!** Study Sheet are included in the Appendix (page 211).

Page 51

A Bright Idea !

If your students really enjoy this form of educational gaming, there are many excellent varieties of ESL Bingo on the market.

This lesson is an economical way to test the waters before making a bigger financial investment in store-bought games.

ZINGO! Game Sheet #1

ZINGO!

A21	C52	P90	E54	U7
F55	L20	D53	H57	B40
A14	S69	L62	Q11	A78
Z48	Z1	G15	G56	B51
V6	Y47	A49	K12	F70

ZINGO!

P95	O65	H28	U19	U70
U72	A50	Q96	T71	V90
Q67	Z70	A78	U14	F26
G40	Y76	A16	V73	P66
Z77	G27	E40	I29	E14

ZINGO! Game Sheet #3

ZINGO!

W5	W74	N80	D53	Y3
E25	T8	Q67	R39	C23
X46	M18	J31	X4	L62
V73	F55	B22	R10	X75
O19	I29	D24	L91	S9

ZINGO! Game Sheet #4

ZINGO!

F84	U19	Z70	E17	C81
R97	T71	N80	G85	V90
S98	X80	L91	T99	O19
D82	X75	A16	Y17	K89
Y76	W18	C60	S69	M18

ZINGO! Game Sheet #5

ZINGO!

U14	I13	E14	H28	Q11
B51	S9	R39	O50	D16
E40	W45	E60	N80	C23
X4	K12	Y17	G40	M34
I15	G56	S98	A15	J13

ZINGO! Game Sheet #6

ZINGO!

G27	Y17	Z77	B22	J88
L33	Q38	A49	V44	X4
O94	M18	U72	T99	H50
E83	R10	W5	Q11	K61
O50	F55	P66	C60	A15

ZINGO! Game Sheet #7

ZINGO!

J59	J30	P37	K12	Q11
B40	F26	N93	G15	I15
S98	K32	I87	O65	V6
Y76	X80	U43	T71	E54
I19	A21	Z48	D82	L20

ZINGO! Game Sheet #8

ZINGO!

L62	H28	B51	U14	Z70
A50	G56	I13	E14	A78
M34	V73	K89	R39	S9
U19	W45	P95	Q67	D16
C23	F84	B22	X4	N80

ZINGO! Game Sheet #9

ZINGO!

M34	C81	D53	I90	E60
N64	M92	J31	S69	T42
R97	K12	H86	O36	X75
U7	W18	P90	A14	F70
E25	J13	Z1	I58	Y47

ZINGO! Game Sheet #10

ZINGO!

I29	Q96	U70	Q11	J30
D24	Y3	E17	O19	X46
G85	B79	V90	C52	W74
S41	N35	M63	E40	L91
R68	H57	A16	G40	T8

ZINGO! Game Sheet #11

ZINGO!

B22	D53	J88	X4	A49
A21	U7	G56	K89	I87
Z1	B51	Z48	H86	F55
Y47	Y3	W5	H57	L91
E54	C23	V6	D24	C52

ZINGO! Game Sheet #12

ZINGO!

I19	I90	Q11	A78	G85
F84	T8	U70	E40	R10
X75	E14	S9	C81	Y76
A15	E83	K12	B79	Q11
A50	P90	J13	Z77	D82

ZINGO! Game Sheet #13

ZINGO!

F70	P95	N93	U19	P66
K12	M92	L20	O65	Q96
V90	S98	Q67	N64	I13
G15	O94	R68	M18	O19
N80	R97	T99	J30	H50

ZINGO! Game Sheet #14

ZINGO!

M34	B40	Z77	A78	B79
O36	P37	I58	L62	S41
A14	N35	M63	E17	X75
K32	K61	J31	R39	L33
J59	Y76	C60	D16	Q38

ZINGO! Game Sheet #15

ZINGO!

H86	S41	M63	O36	U72
M92	A14	G40	W5	I90
V44	D53	O36	Y47	T42
L62	G27	S98	U14	E60
F84	Z77	K61	I58	J59

A14	B40	C60	D16	E17
F70	G15	H50	I13	J30
K12	L20	M18	N80	O19
P90	Q11	R10	S9	T8
U7	V6	W5	X4	Y3
Z1	A21	B22	C23	D24

Chapter 4. **ZINGO!** Game Chips #2

E25	F26	G27	H28	I29
J31	K32	L33	M34	N35
O36	P37	Q38	R39	S41
T42	U43	V44	W45	X46
Y47	Z48	A49	B51	C52
D53	E54	F55	G56	H57

I58	J59	K61	L62	M63
N64	O65	P66	Q67	R68
S69	T71	U72	V73	W74
X75	Y76	Z77	A78	B79
C81	D82	E83	F84	G85
H86	I87	J88	K89	L91

M92	N93	O94	P95	Q96
R97	S98	T99	U19	V90
W18	X80	Y17	Z70	A16
E60	I15	O50	U14	G40
J13	K12	Q11	E14	E40
I90	I19	A15	A50	U70

Chapter 5. **Exact Change** Directions

OBJECTIVE:

To make students more comfortable with handling U.S. currency.

HOW TO PREPARE FOR THIS LESSON:

Photocopy enough **Exact Change** Study Sheets and **Exact Change** Worksheets for each student and yourself.

Photocopy and cut out the **1-2-3- Write!** Money Game Chips (pages 46-48). Photocopy and cut out the one, five, ten, twenty, fifty, and one hundred dollar bills and their accompanying coins (pages 237-242).

Go over the study sheets as a class, then have your students do the worksheets individually as a warm-up to this lesson. This will help you guage how comfortable each student is with U.S. currency and help you divide the class more evenly into teams of varied proficiencies.

Divide the class into two teams. One person from Team A will be the Customer and one person from Team B will be the Cashier. If you only have three students, have each student play for himself or herself.

NOW BEGIN:

Place the bills and coins on the table between the Cashier and the Customer. Place the game chips,

---

Prior to this Lesson:

Depending on the level of your students, it might be best to complete:

- 1-2-3 Write!

- ZINGO!

prior to doing this lesson.

Note:

This lesson doesn't really lend itself well to large classes with many teams (unless you are team teaching), since you, The Teacher, need to be constantly on hand to closely supervise the players throughout the activity.

Chapter 5. **Exact Change**   Directions

Page 72

**Save A Tree
Save Some Time**

Photocopy and cover both sides of your **1-2-3 Write!** U.S. Currency Game Chips and the U.S. Currency with clear packing tape before cutting them into individual pieces. This will make them more durable for repeated use.

Collect the game chips and currency at the end of each lesson and place them in labeled envelopes for future use.

face down, on the table. Take a seat next to the Cashier to check for mistakes.

The Cashier chooses a game chip at random from the pile and, without showing it to the Customer, reads the amount that is written. The Cashier must read the number loudly and clearly enough for the Customer to hear it. But he/she doesn't have to say it slowly. The Customer may ask the Cashier to repeat the amount only once.

If the Cashier reads the amount incorrectly, the Customer automatically gets to keep the game chip, his/her team earns a point, and the round is over.

If the Cashier reads the amount correctly, the Customer must then pull from the pile of money on the table and pay the Cashier exactly that amount—not a penny over or under. If the Customer is able to do this, he/she gets to keep the game chip, thus earning a point for their team.

If the Customer does not pay the exact amount, the Cashier gets to keep the game chip, thus earning a point for his/her team.

When each round is over, a new player is chosen for each team. If the previous player for Team A was the Cashier, the new player is now the Customer and vice versa.

Chapter 5. Exact Change — Directions

You, The Teacher, are responsible for making sure the Cashier reads the game chips correctly and that the Customer pays the exact amount.

You should also point out, when needed, more efficient ways to use the coins. For example, if a Customer uses a one dollar bill and six pennies to pay for something that costs $1.06, show the Customer that they could simply use one penny and one nickel for the change instead.

VARIATIONS:

You may already be thinking of alternative ways to customize this basic lesson to your specific class. One idea, to make it more challenging for more advanced classes, is to give the Customer the option of paying the exact amount or over-paying and requiring the Cashier to accurately pay back the difference (the change).

For example, if the Cashier picks up a game chip for $18.54 and the Customer pays $20.00, the Cashier must pull from the pile of money on the table and give the exact change of $1.46 to earn the point. If the Cashier gives back the incorrect change, the Customer earns the point.

It might be a good idea to bring a calculator to help you check the accuracy of everyone's math.

A Good Precursor to:

- Grocery Shopping

You may find that a lesson purely on numbers fails to engage students as much as when the numbers suddenly become about money—even fake money.

Once your students are comfortable with currency, you might come up with other games and uses for the U.S. Currency located in the Appendix (page 237). The **Grocery Shopping** lesson (page 163) takes the Customer/Cashier dynamic a step further.

Exact Change Study Sheet #1

One Dollar Bill

Five Dollar Bill

Ten Dollar Bill

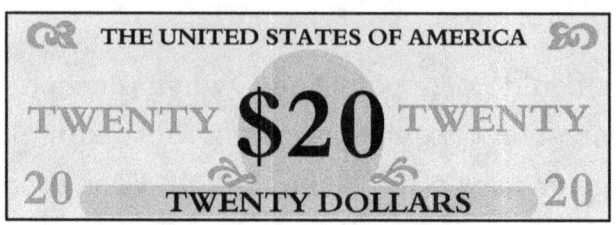
Twenty Dollar Bill

Fifty Dollar Bill

One Hundred Dollar Bill

 Penny  Nickel  Dime  Quarter

Two Dollar Bill

One Thousand Dollar Bill

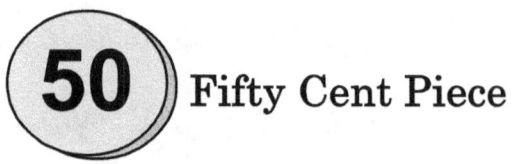 Fifty Cent Piece

 One Dollar Coin

Exact Change   Study Sheet #2

N = P P P P P

D = N N

D = P P P P P P P P P P

D = P P P P P N

Q = N N N N N

Q = D N D

Q = (25 P's)

Q = P P P P N D N

$1 = Q Q Q Q

$1 = D D D D D D D D D D

$1 = Q D N N N P P Q D N N P P P P

$10 = $5 $5

Exact Change Worksheet

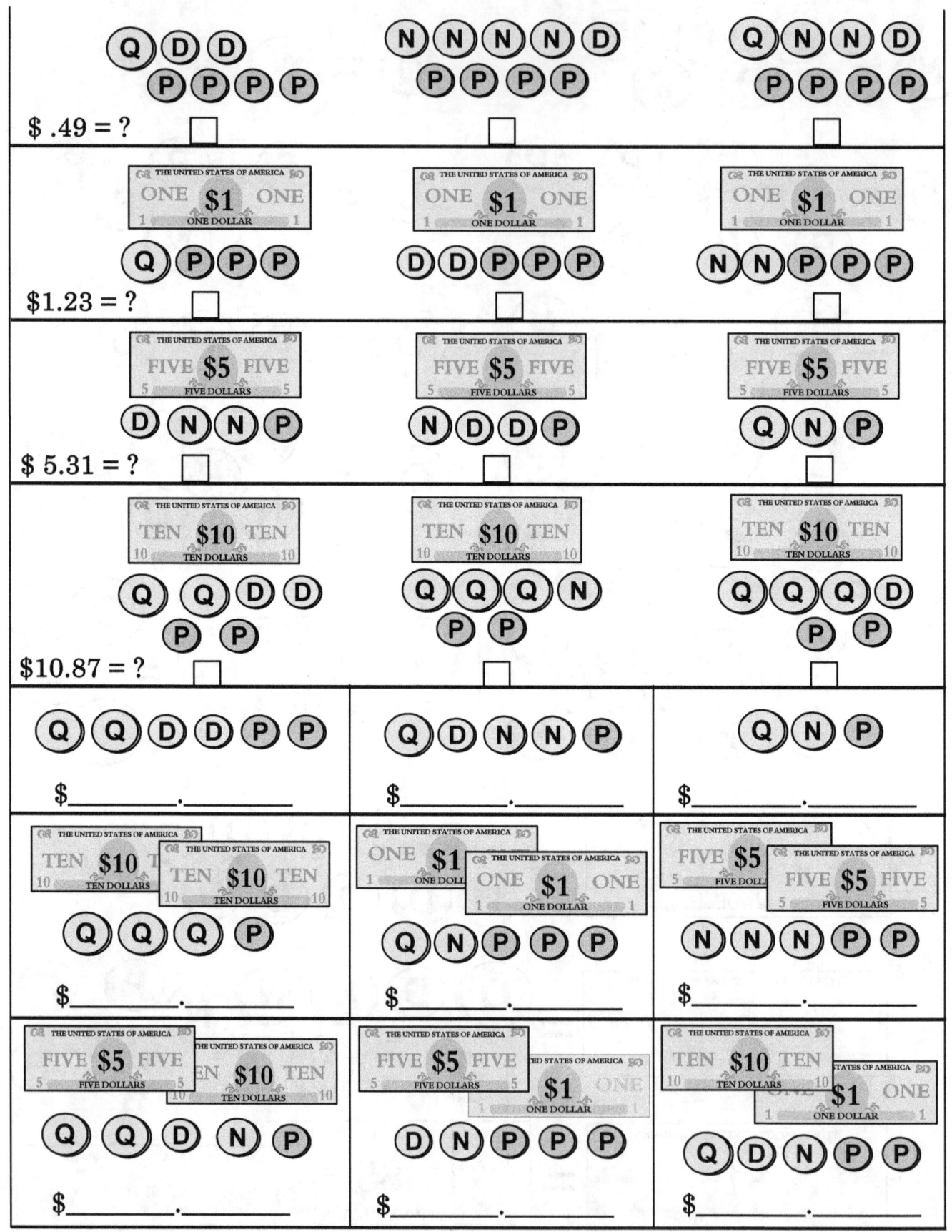

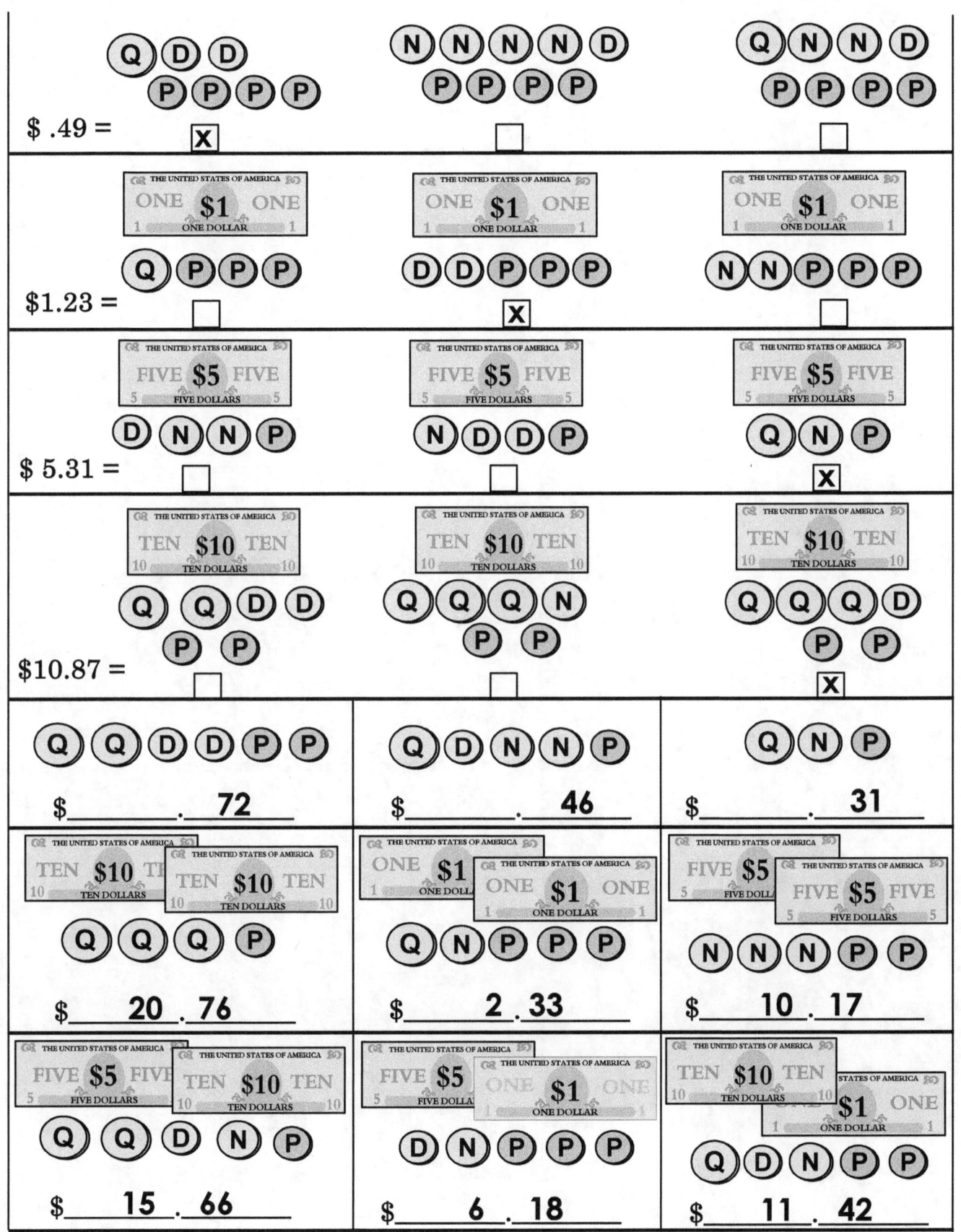

Chapter 6. Map of the United States — Directions

OBJECTIVE:

To get the class familiar with the map of the United States and learn the abbreviation of each state.

HOW TO PREPARE FOR THIS LESSON:

Photocopy one **Map of the United States** Study Sheet and one **Map of the United States** Completed for each student and yourself.

Photocopy one **Map of the United States** Blank for each pair of students.

Divide the class into partners. If you have an odd number of students, make one group of three students. Give each pair (or trio) a **Map of the United States** Blank sheet.

Go over the study sheet as a class to make sure they know how to pronounce all the states correctly.

NOW BEGIN:

Make it clear that they should complete the maps using abbreviations rather than writing out the entire state names. Your role at this point is to simply go around the class and check off the states that they've filled in correctly. Offer no other clues

---

A Good Precursor to:

○ May I Ask Who's Calling?

○ Talking Trivia
 - U.S. Geography (page 183)

Learning the abbreviations for various states can come in handy when taking messages from callers from the United States.

Chapter 6. Map of the United States — Directions

Page 80

Cheater Alert!

Make sure there is no cheating, as bilingual dictionaries often include maps in them.

or help. The first pair to finish their map correctly wins.

Hand each student a completed map at the end of class, since the blank maps used during the lesson will probably get messy and become hard to read.

This lesson is intended to be more of a light, fairly quick activity—not the main focus of the class. There is no actual grammar being taught here, but it's useful for students to have a fairly good idea of where someone's calling from when they take a message or to be able to identify where someone is from when making small talk.

If possible, try to pair students who have traveled to the United States with students who haven't, to keep some balance.

For interactive, on-line activities, try:

- ProfessorMelonhead.com/Map_UnitedStates.html
- ProfessorMelonhead.com/Spelling_States.html

Map of the United States — Completed

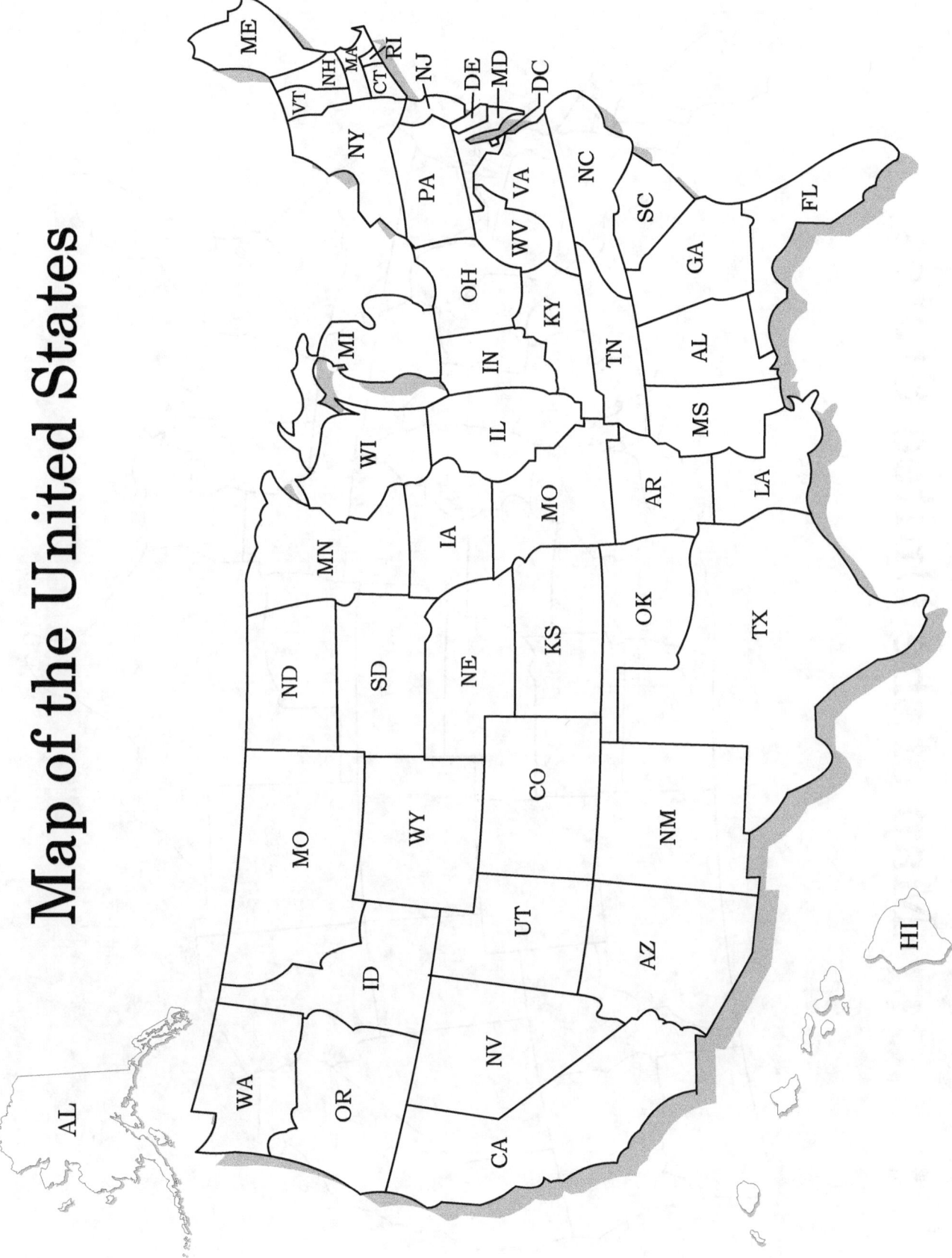

FUN, QUICK & EASY — Game-Based Activities for Teachers of Adult ESL

Map of the United States   Blank

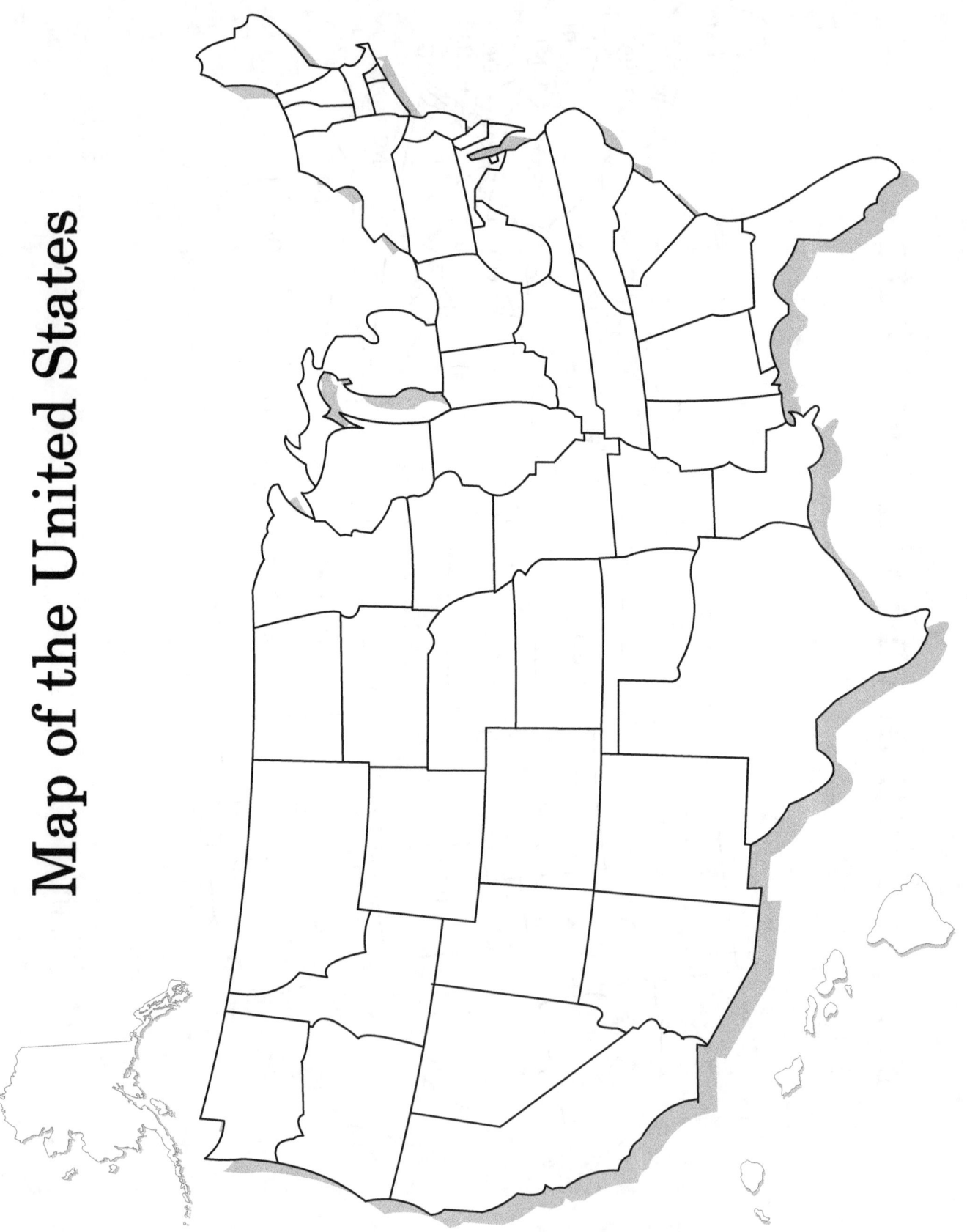

Page 82   FUN, QUICK & EASY   Game-Based Activities for Teachers of Adult ESL

Map of the United States — Study Sheet

States	Abbreviations	States	Abbreviations
ALABAMA	AL	MONTANA	MT
ALASKA	AK	NEBRASKA	NE
ARIZONA	AZ	NEVADA	NV
ARKANSAS	AR	NEW HAMPSHIRE	NH
CALIFORNIA	CA	NEW JERSEY	NJ
COLORADO	CO	NEW MEXICO	NM
CONNECTICUT	CT	NEW YORK	NY
DELAWARE	DE	NORTH CAROLINA	NC
FLORIDA	FL	NORTH DAKOTA	ND
GEORGIA	GA	OHIO	OH
HAWAII	HI	OKLAHOMA	OK
IDAHO	ID	OREGON	OR
ILLINOIS	IL	PENNSYLVANIA	PA
INDIANA	IN	RHODE ISLAND	RI
IOWA	IA	SOUTH CAROLINA	SC
KANSAS	KS	SOUTH DAKOTA	SD
KENTUCKY	KY	TENNESSEE	TN
LOUISIANA	LA	TEXAS	TX
MAINE	ME	UTAH	UT
MARYLAND	MD	VERMONT	VT
MASSACHUSETTS	MA	VIRGINIA	VA
MICHIGAN	MI	WASHINGTON	WA
MINNESOTA	MN	WEST VIRGINIA	WV
MISSISSIPPI	MS	WISCONSIN	WI
MISSOURI	MO	WYOMING	WY
		*DISTRICT OF COLUMBIA	DC

* Washington DC is not a state. It is a district and the capital of the United States.

Chapter 7. May I Ask Who's Calling? Directions

OBJECTIVE:

Taking and leaving simple telephone messages.

HOW TO PREPARE FOR THIS LESSON:

Photocopy the **May I Ask Who's Calling?** Game Cards and enough **May I Ask Who's Calling?** Study Sheets #1 through #4 for each student and yourself.

Go over the study sheets, paying particular attention to Study Sheet #4. Have the students work in partners to try to get through as much of the dialogue as possible without looking at it.

NOW BEGIN:

Have one student, the Secretary, go to the board. Have another student, the Caller, choose a game card at random and sit with their back to the board so they cannot see it. (Part of the challenge of phone messages is that you cannot see the person you're talking to.)

Using the same format as Study Sheet #4, the Caller and the Secretary must try to communicate clearly enough so that the information the Caller is trying to give is accurately recorded by the Secretary.

Prior to this Lesson:

Depending on the level of your students, it might be best to complete:

- 1-2-3 Write!

- ZINGO!

- Map of the United States

prior to doing this lesson.

Chapter 7.   May I Ask Who's Calling?   Directions

Page 86

An Anecdote:

I had a student in Germany who often took calls from English speakers. Usually, he would have to ask them to speak more slowly. Despite his request, they would usually continue speaking at their normal pace.

Finally, he would just start speaking German at his normal pace to turn the tables on them. Then, when he repeated his request in English for them to speak slower, they would.

You may want to offer this advice to any of your frustrated students who often face this problem, especially to those unsung heroes of most companies, the Administrative Assistants.

When they have completed the exercise, the Caller can turn around and compare what is on his/her game card with what is written on the board. If the Caller finds any mistakes, he/she can repeat that information to see if the Secretary can find his/her error and correct it.

During this exercise, the rest of the class is not to help the Secretary until the round is over. The phone call should only involve the Caller and the Secretary.

When the round is over, choose a new Caller and a new Secretary and start again with a new game card.

Variations:

A more advanced version of this lesson, **May I Ask Who's Calling? Part 2**, is located in the Appendix (page 232).

If you do not have access to a whiteboard or chalkboard, Phone Message Sheets are provided in the Appendix (page 231). These can also be useful if you want to have the class do partner work at their desk.

May I Ask Who's Calling?   Study Sheet #1

Getting the Name

What's your name?
May I ask who's calling?
Can I have your name (please)?
Could you tell me your name please?

Getting Accurate Information

Could you spell your (first / last) name please?
Could you repeat that (please)?
Could you speak more slowly please?
Could you speak more loudly please?

Getting the Address

What's your address?
May I have your address?
Could you tell me your address (please)?

Getting the Telephone Number

What's your telephone number?
May I have your telephone number (please)?

Taking a Message

Mr. Jones is not in. May I take a message?
Mr. Jones is not in (his office). Would you like to leave a message?
Mr. Jones is in a meeting. Would you like his voice mail?
Mr. Jones is at lunch. Can I have him call you back?

Making Appointments

Ms. Smith is booked today. Can she see you tomorrow?
Ms. Smith is busy today. Would you like to make an appointment for tomorrow?
Today is not convenient for Ms. Smith. Can I schedule you for tomorrow?

Putting a Caller on Hold

Mr. Johnson's line is busy. Would you like to hold?
Mr. Johnson is on another line. May I put you on hold?
Mr. Johnson's office, hold please.

Connecting a Caller

Thank you for waiting. I'll put you through.
Thank you for holding. I'll connect you now.

Options for a Caller on Hold

Ms. Hall's line is still busy. Do you want to continue holding?
Ms. Hall's line is still busy. If you'd like to leave your name and number,
   I'll have her call you back.

May I Ask Who's Calling?   Study Sheet #2

Standard Address Abbreviations

St.	Street		
Dr.	Drive	Cir.	Circle
Rd.	Road	Ct.	Court
Ave.	Avenue	Ln.	Lane
Blvd.	Boulevard	Mt.	Mount
Ter.	Terrace	Hwy.	Highway
Pl.	Place	Fwy.	Freeway

Buildings

Bsmt.	Basement	Plz.	Plaza
Apt.	Apartment	Ctr.	Center

Office

Br.	Branch	Bldg.	Building
Fl.	Floor	Ste.	Suite
Dept.	Department	Ext.	Extension

Direction

N	North	NW	Northwest
S	South	NE	Northeast
E	East	SW	Southwest
W	West	SE	Southeast

May I Ask Who's Calling?   Study Sheet #3

Jennifer Johnson
2268 SE Beech Blvd
Baton Rouge, LA 70806
(225) 821-3574

Jennifer – First / Given Name

Johnson – Last / Family Name

2268 SE Beech Blvd – Street Address

Baton Rouge – City

LA – State (always abbreviated)

70806 – Zip Code

(225) – Area Code

925-2576 – Telephone Number

May I Ask Who's Calling?   Study Sheet #4

RING! RING!

Q: Squeaky Clean Soap Company. How can I help you?
A: I'd like to have one of your catalogs mailed to me.

Q: Certainly. What is your **first name**, please?
A: My **first name** is Jennifer.

Q: Could you repeat that please?
A: Sure, Jennifer.

Q: How do you spell that please?
A: J...E...N...N...I...F...E...R.

Q: Thank you. And your **last name** please?
A: Johnson.

Q: May I have your **street address** please?
A: My **street address** is 2268 SE Beech Blvd.

Q: Could you repeat that more slowly please?
A: Certainly. 2...2...6...8...South...East.....Beech.....Blvd.

Q: Thank you. And your **city** and **state**?
A: Baton Rouge, Louisiana.

Q: Okay, and what's your **zip code** please?
A: It's 70806.

Q: **Area code** and **telephone number** please?
A: My **number** is **area code** (225) 925-2576.

Q: You can expect your catalog to arrive in 10 business days.
A: Thank you.

Chapter 7. **May I Ask Who's Calling?** Game Cards #1

Cary Grant 673 N Avenue 1889 Los Angeles, CA 90032 (323) 976-2639	**Marilyn Monroe** 215 S Park Pl Birmingham, AL 89567 (205) 264-2587
Rock Hudson 3926 E Tournament Dr Houston, TX 77069 (281) 454-6249	**Katherine Hepburn** 73 NW 54th St Washington, DC 20001 (202) 482-5729
Clark Gable 735 SE 7th Ave New York, NY 10001 (212) 949-3349	**Bette Davis** 801 SW 53rd St Minneapolis, MN 55419 (612) 525-7473
Fred Astaire 3538 N Turret Way Boise, ID 83708 (208) 485-5254	**Sophia Loren** 3925 N Nordica Ave Chicago, IL 60634 (773) 725-3253
Gene Kelly 6574 New Britain Ave Hartford, CT 06014 (860) 347-8563	**Lucille Ball** 6274 Ridgefield Rd Philadelphia, PA 19153 (215) 856-3474

Jack Lemmon 137 Gardens Dr Springfield, MA 01119 (413) 783-7458	**Cyd Charisse** 400 Wilma Cir Miami, FL 33404 (561) 845-6875
Montgomery Cliff 2740 A Ave NE Cedar Rapids, IA 52402 (319) 365-9643	**Kim Novak** 921 Highway 44 Brookhaven, MS 39601 (601) 823-1169
James Dean North 145th Street Seattle, WA 98168 (206) 568-1725	**Elizabeth Taylor** 5920 Leith Rd Baltimore, MD 21231 (410) 604-8246
Tony Curtis 316 NW Hartwell Pl Portland, OR 97228 (503) 365-9643	**Grace Kelly** 2125 S. Summit Ave Sioux Falls, SD 57106 (605) 257-9743
Marlon Brando 6834 Fletcher Ave Lincoln, NE 68521 (402) 758-1347	**Dorothy Dandridge** 829 Waconda Rd Chattanooga, TN 37419 (423) 584-1057

Humphrey Bogart 4318 Doonesbury Dr Austin, TX 78751 (512) 685-4485	**Anna May Wong** 514 Mabelvale Pike Little Rock, AR 72211 (501) 347-6044
Bing Crosby 6874 E Vermillion Dr Baton Rouge, LA 70812 (225) 865-1776	**Lauren Bacall** 875 S Chestnut Hill Rd Albany, NY 12204 (518) 874-6457
Sammy Davis Jr. 2128 Alverson Ave Providence, RI 02908 (401) 284-3763	**Ingrid Bergman** 1468 N Renaissance Ln New Brunswick, NJ 08902 (732) 448-6710
James Cagney 3684 W Royal Crest Cir Las Vegas, NV 89147 (702) 658-1478	**Joan Crawford** 2586 N 44th Pl Phoenix, AZ 85085 (602) 369-2568
Jimmy Stewart 7468 Pebble Dr Atlanta, GA 30345 (678) 854-7430	**Judy Garland** 79 Arnold Palmer Dr Raleigh, NC 27614 (919) 168-5571

Chapter 8. Architect Directions

OBJECTIVE:

To introduce students to prepositions of place.

HOW TO PREPARE FOR THIS LESSON:

Photocopy enough **Architect** Study Sheets for each student and yourself.

Photocopy and cut out one sheet of **Architect** Game Pieces for each team. Photocopy one **Architect** Game Card for each team. Make sure that each team has a different game card.

The team whose **Architect** Game Pieces most closely resemble their **Architect** Game Card wins.

NOW BEGIN:

Depending on your class size, divide the class into groups of 3 or 4. Try to have the same number of students in each group if possible.

Each team will have one Describer. Each Describer gets their own game card. Only they get to see the **Architect** Game Card.

Each team has one or two Builders. These people never see the **Architect** Game Card, nor do they

---

A Good Precursor to:

- Preposition Bluff

- Where's the Post Office?

Note

This lesson is intended for larger classes. However, it can be played with a minimum of 6 people—2 teams of three people:

- 1 Describer
- 1 Messenger
- 1 Builder

This game is more fun if there are at least three teams competing.

Chapter 8. **Architect** Directions

Save A Tree
Save Some Time

Photocopy and cover both sides of the **Architect** Game Pieces sheets with clear packing tape before cutting them into pieces. This will make them more durable for repeated use.

Collect the game pieces at the end of each lesson and place them in a labeled envelope for future use.

Business Relevance

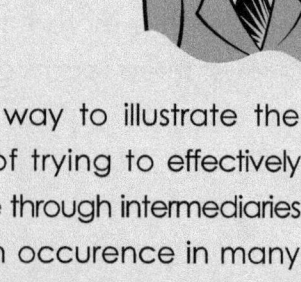

This is a fun way to illustrate the challenges of trying to effectively communicate through intermediaries—a common occurence in many business situations—particularly with the rising trend in outsourcing.

ever speak directly to the Describer. They are the only people who handle the **Architect** Game Pieces.

Each team has one Messenger. The Messenger communicates between the Describer and the Builder(s). The Messenger never sees the **Architect** Game Cards, nor does he/she ever handle the **Architect** Game Pieces.

Provide each team of Builders with their own **Architect** Game Pieces and a flat surface to assemble them on, preferably far from the other teams of Builders.

Hand each Describer their own **Architect** Game Card and send them out of the room or somewhere far from the rest of the players. Give them about five minutes to carefully study their game card.

After the five minutes are up, the Describers must put down their game cards—face down—before describing their picture to the Messenger. Both the Messenger and Describer must keep their hands behind their backs whenever they speak to each other. When the Messenger leaves, the Describer is then free to go back to their game card and continue studying it until the Messenger returns.

The Messenger then goes to the Builders and repeats

Chapter 8. **Architect** Directions

the description of the picture. The Messenger must keep their hands behind their back when speaking to the Builder(s).

Based on the information given by the Messenger, the Builder(s) begin assembling the games pieces. At no time may the Messenger touch or gesture towards the game pieces. Any questions the Builders have must go through the Messenger.

You can either have the teams race the clock or race each other. For an intermediate level class or higher, a 20-30 minute time limit should do. Add an additional 10-15 minutes for lower level classes.

Either way, when the time is up, the Builders can no longer touch the game pieces. The Describers place the game cards next to the work the Builders have done.

It's always fun for the class to see how close—or not so close—they got to the picture. It's also fun to go around the room to see how the other teams progressed.

A Bright Idea !

If you plan on using this activity often, consider investing in Legos. There are versions with little plastic windows, fencing, roofs, etc. in various colors.

Just assemble a variety of simple but similar houses before class and provide each team with the duplicate Lego pieces to reproduce them (plus a few extra pieces thrown in to keep it interesting).

Legos are a lightweight, durable alternative that you can use over and over again.

Architect   Study Sheet

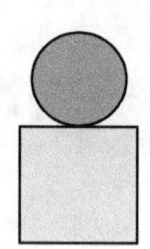

The circle is **on** the square.
The circle is **over** the square.
The circle is **above** the square.

The square is **under** the circle.
The square is **underneath** the circle.
The square is **below** the circle.

The circle is **next to** the square.
The circle is **to the right of** the square.
The circle is **beside** the square.

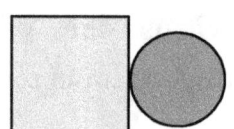

The square is **next to** the circle.
The square is **to the left of** the circle.
The square is **beside** the circle.

The triangle is **in front of** the square.
The square is **behind** the triangle.

The triangle is **on** the square.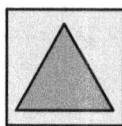

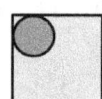 The circle is **in the upper right corner of** the square.

The circle is **in the upper left corner of** the square.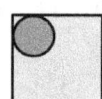

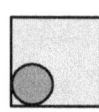 The circle is **in the lower right corner of** the square.

The circle is **in the lower left corner of** the square.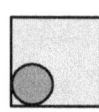

Page 98   **Fun, Quick & Easy**   Game-Based Activities for Teachers of Adult ESL

Chapter 8. **Architect** Game Pieces

Architect   Game Card #1

Page 100   **Fun, Quick & Easy**   Game-Based Activities for Teachers of Adult ESL

Architect Game Card #2

Page 101

Architect   Game Card #3

Page 102   FUN, QUICK & EASY   Game-Based Activities for Teachers of Adult ESL

Architect   Game Card #4

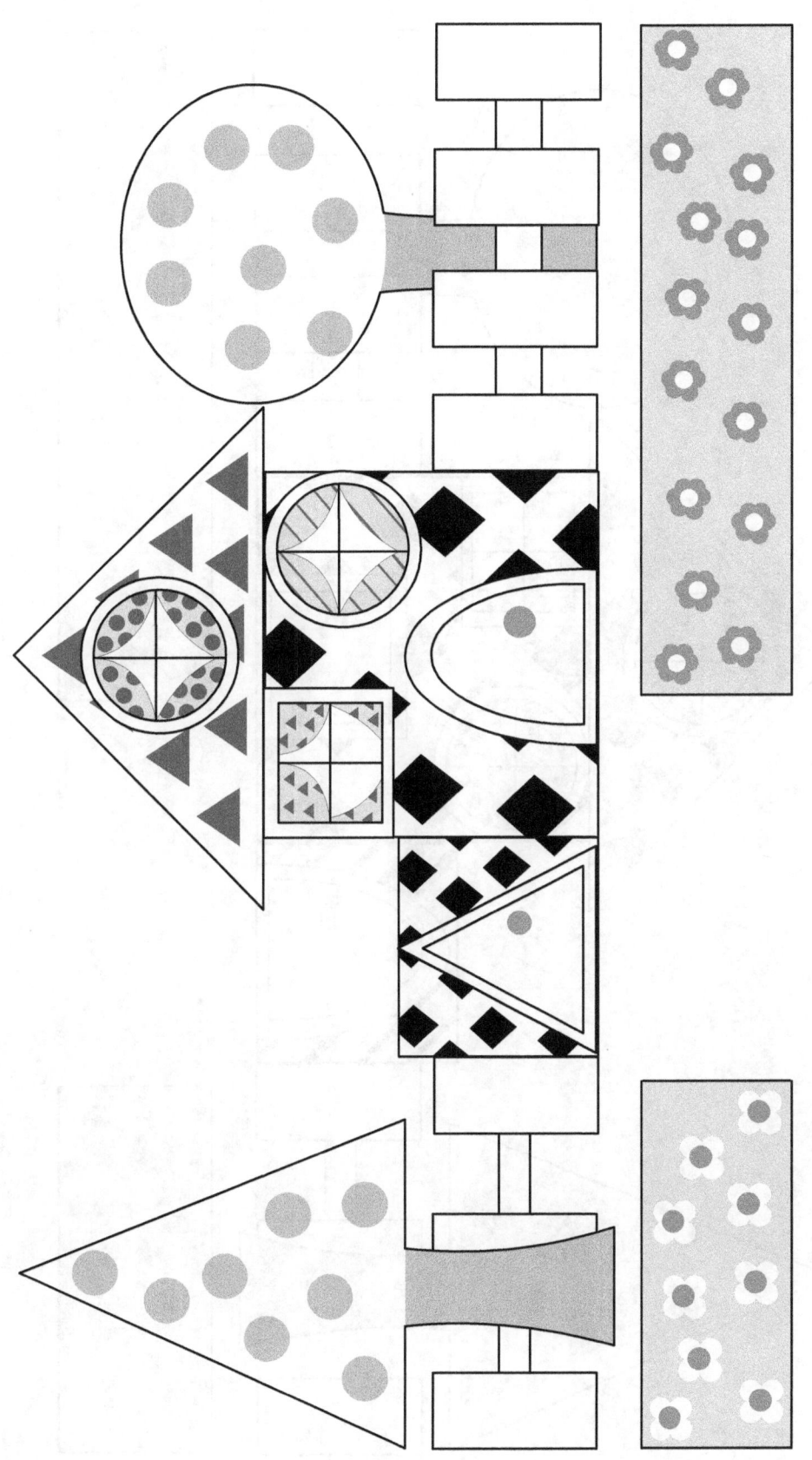

FUN, QUICK & EASY   Game-Based Activities for Teachers of Adult ESL

Architect Game Card #5

Page 104 **Fun, Quick & Easy** Game-Based Activities for Teachers of Adult ESL

Architect Game Card #6

FUN, QUICK & EASY   Game-Based Activities for Teachers of Adult ESL

Architect   Game Card #7

Page 106   **Fun, Quick & Easy**   Game-Based Activities for Teachers of Adult ESL

Chapter 9. **Preposition Bluff** Directions

OBJECTIVE:

To reinforce the understanding of prepositions.

HOW TO PREPARE FOR THIS LESSON:

Photocopy and cut out the **Preposition Bluff** Game Cards.

NOW BEGIN:

Spread the game cards, face down, in the center of the table. Explain that on each card there are 4 sentences; 2 are grammatically correct and the other 2 are grammatically incorrect.

Divide the class into 2 teams. Player A (from Team A) chooses a game card and reads one of the sentences. Player B (from Team B) must correctly say if the sentence is grammatically correct or incorrect to earn the point. If Player B answers incorrectly, Team A earns the point.

If the sentence is grammatically incorrect and Player B says so, he/she must say the sentence correctly, replacing the incorrect preposition with the correct one to earn the point. Otherwise, Team A keeps the game card and earns the point.

A player from Team B then reads to a player from Team A for the next round. Whichever team has the most cards at the end of the game wins.

Page 107

Prior to this Lesson:

Depending on the level of your students, it might be best to complete:

○ Architect

prior to doing this lesson.

A Bright Idea !

If you only have 3 students, have everyone play for themselves and just go around the table one at a time.

Student A reads to Student B, Student B reads to Student C, and Student C reads to Student A.

This is fun for the class and also effective.

Page 108   Chapter 9.   **Preposition Bluff**   Game Cards #1

| TRUE | I saw it **on** television. | TRUE | I have been married **for** 8 years. |
| | I read about it **in** the newspaper. | | I have been awake **since** 2:00 A.M. |

| FALSE | I saw it **in** television. | FALSE | I have been awake **until** 2:00 A.M. |
| | I read about it **on** the newspaper. | | I have been married **since** 8 years. |

| TRUE | She found it **on** the map. | TRUE | We came to the meeting **by** train. |
| | He explained it **in** his report. | | She completed the journey **on** foot. |

| FALSE | She found it **in** the map. | FALSE | We came to the meeting **on** train. |
| | He explained it **on** his report. | | She completed the journey **by** foot. |

| TRUE | We live **on** Maple Avenue. | TRUE | He is **from** the Sales Department. |
| | The bus will leave **in** 20 minutes. | | She is the head **of** Operations. |

| FALSE | We live **at** Maple Avenue. | FALSE | He is **of** the Sales Department. |
| | The bus will leave **at** 20 minutes. | | She is the head **from** Operations. |

| TRUE | Ms. Jones is talking **on** the phone. | TRUE | I will arrive **in** an hour or two. |
| | Julio is never **at** home on Friday nights. | | I'll meet you **at** home in an hour. |

| FALSE | Ms. Jones is talking **at** the phone. | FALSE | I will arrive **by** an hour or two. |
| | Julio is never **in** home on Friday nights. | | I'll meet you **in** home in an hour. |

| TRUE | I am interested **in** buying a new car. | TRUE | I will sleep **for** two hours. |
| | Congratulations! I'm so happy **for** you. | | Can you finish this **for** me? I have to go. |

| FALSE | I am interested **for** buying a new car. | FALSE | I will sleep **until** two hours. |
| | Congratulations! I'm so happy **with** you. | | Can you finish this **with** me? I have to go. |

Chapter 9. **Preposition Bluff** Game Cards #2

TRUE	The meeting is **at** 2 o'clock. We're scheduled to leave **at** 8 PM.	TRUE	I was born **in** June. I was born **on** June 1st, 1965.
FALSE	The meeting is **on** 2 o'clock. We're scheduled to leave **in** 8 PM.	FALSE	I was born **on** June. I was born **in** June 1st, 1965.
TRUE	I have worked here **for** 5 years. I have worked here **since** last May.	TRUE	I work **for** ABC Company. I work **in** The HR Department.
FALSE	I have worked here **since** 5 years. I have worked here **for** last May.	FALSE	I work **in** ABC Company. I work **at** The HR Department.
TRUE	Are you busy **at** the moment? Are you free this afternoon? (no prep)	TRUE	I am responsible **for** this project. I am in charge **of** the new project.
FALSE	Are you busy **in** the moment? Are you free **for** this afternoon?	FALSE	I am responsible **of** this project. I am in charge **for** the new project.
TRUE	She lives **on** the island of Kauai. Turn left **at** the next corner.	TRUE	My train will arrive **at** noon. My train will depart **at** midnight.
FALSE	She lives **in** the island of Kauai. Turn left **on** the next corner.	FALSE	My train will arrive **on** noon. My train will depart **in** midnight.
TRUE	I was born **on** May 1st, 1965. I was born **in** May.	TRUE	Someone's **at** the door. Please hang that picture **on** the wall.
FALSE	I was born **in** May 1st, 1965. I was born **on** May.	FALSE	Someone's **in** the door. Please hang that picture **at** the wall.

TRUE The reports will be ready **in** 2 days. We should have the results **on** Tuesday.	TRUE I'll be home **in** three days. I'll be there **in** an hour.
FALSE The reports will be ready **at** 2 days. We should have the results **at** Tuesday.	FALSE I'll be home **at** three days. I'll be there **on** an hour.
TRUE I have lived here **for** 8 years. I have lived here **since** last year.	TRUE I work **for** XYZ Inc. I work **in** The Sales Department.
FALSE I have lived here **since** 8 years. I have lived here **in** last year.	FALSE I work **in** XYZ Company. I work **at** The Sales Department.
TRUE Are you free **for** dinner? Are you free this weekend? (no prep)	TRUE I am in charge **of** quality control. I am responsible **for** new employees.
FALSE Are you free **at** dinner? Are you free **for** this weekend?	FALSE I am in charge **for** quality control. I am responsible **of** new employees.
TRUE I booked a flight **for** next Tuesday. I reserved a meeting room **for** 8 PM.	TRUE The bus will arrive **at** 11AM. The bus will leave **at** 2 o'clock.
FALSE I booked a flight **on** next Tuesday. reserved a meeting room **on** 8 PM.	FALSE The bus will arrive **on** 11 AM. The bus will leave **on** 2 o'clock.
TRUE He was waiting **at** the bus stop. Sign your name **at** the top of the form.	TRUE I spent two weeks **in** Madrid, Spain. I love to work **in** my garage at night.
FALSE He was waiting **on** the bus stop. Sign your name **on** the top of the form.	FALSE I spent two weeks **at** Madrid, Spain. I love to work **at** my garage at night.

Chapter 9. **Preposition Bluff** Game Cards #4

| TRUE | Our company was founded **in** 1953. | TRUE | Submit the invoices **on** June 15th. |
| | I was hired **on** May 15th, 2001. | | I worked there 4 years ago. **(no prep)** |

| FALSE | Our company was founded **on** 1953. | FALSE | Submit the invoices **in** June 15th. |
| | I was hired **at** May 15th, 2001. | | I worked there **since** 4 years ago. |

| TRUE | We'll be back from lunch **in** an hour. | TRUE | Turn left **at** the next intersection. |
| | I hate standing **in** long lines. | | You have a stain **on** your shirt. |

| FALSE | We'll be back from lunch **at** an hour. | FALSE | Turn left **on** the next intersection. |
| | I hate standing **on** long lines. | | You have a stain **in** your shirt. |

| TRUE | I study every Friday night. **(no prep)** | TRUE | There's a spider **on** the ceiling. |
| | We meet **on** Monday mornings. | | They have a cabin **in** the mountains. |

| FALSE | I study **at** every Friday night. | FALSE | There's a spider **in** the ceiling. |
| | We meet **in** Monday mornings. | | They have a cabin **on** the mountains. |

| TRUE | Is someone **in** the kitchen? | TRUE | I agree **with** you. |
| | Please put the folders **on** my desk. | | That makes sense **to** me. |

| FALSE | Is someone **at** the kitchen? | FALSE | I agree **to** you. |
| | Please put the folders **at** my desk. | | That makes sense **for** me. |

| TRUE | We had a picnic **on** the lawn. | TRUE | What will you do **on/at** Christmas? |
| | We had a picnic **in** the yard. | | What will you do **on** Christmas Day? |

| FALSE | We had a picnic **in** the lawn. | FALSE | What will you do **in** Christmas? |
| | We had a picnic **on** the yard. | | What will you do **at** Christmas Day? |

Chapter 9. **Preposition Bluff** Game Cards #5

TRUE Must we work **on** New Years Day? I usually wrap gifts **on** Christmas Eve.	TRUE Mr. Jones is busy **at** the moment. We both arrived **at** the same time.
FALSE Must we work **at** New Year's Day? I usually wrap gifts **at** Christmas Eve.	FALSE Mr. Jones is busy **in** the moment. We both arrived **by** the same time.
TRUE I stayed up late last night. (no prep) They stay up late every night. (no prep)	TRUE I go to church **on** Sunday mornings. I'll see you next Thursday **at** 3 o'clock.
FALSE I stayed up late **at** last night. They stay up late **on** every night.	FALSE I go to church **in** Sunday mornings. I'll see you next Thursday **on** 3 o'clock.
TRUE The room is **at** the end of the hall. The office is **at** the end of the hall.	TRUE Please put the food **on** the table. The switch is **at** the top of the stairs.
FALSE The room is **on** the end of the hall. The office is **in** the end of the hall.	FALSE Please put the food **at** the table. The switch is **on** the top of the stairs.
TRUE We visited Italy last Winter. (no prep) That dog always barks **at** midnight.	TRUE What will you do **in** the future? Disco music started **in** the 70s.
FALSE We visited Italy **in** last Winter. That dog always barks **on** midnight.	FALSE What will you do **on** the future? Disco music started **at** the 70s.
TRUE They got married last year. (no prep) We arrived at 6 o'clock **in** the morning.	TRUE We like to ski **at** night. I'll see you **on** Friday night.
FALSE They got married **on** this year. We arrived at 6 o'clock **at** the morning.	FALSE We like to ski **in** the night. I'll see you **at** Friday night.

Chapter 9.   **Preposition Bluff**   Game Cards #6

Page 113

TRUE Please get some eggs **at** the store. Please get some eggs **on** your way home.	TRUE He had a stain **on** his tie. Buy your train tickets **at** the next window.
FALSE Please get some eggs **in** the store. Please get some eggs **by** your way home.	FALSE He had a stain **in** his tie. Buy your train tickets **in** the next window.
TRUE She looked out **of** the window. I'm so sick and tired **of** working!	TRUE They get up early **in** the morning. Put the ice cream back **in** the freezer.
FALSE She looked out **from** the window. I'm so sick and tired **from** working!	FALSE They get up early **at** the morning. Put the ice cream back **on** the freezer.
TRUE Sally paid **with** her new credit card. Sally applied **for** a new credit card.	TRUE Please be **on** time for class. I haven't practiced **in** over 3 months.
FALSE Sally paid **from** her new credit card. Sally applied **with** a new credit card.	FALSE Please be **in** time for class. I haven't practiced **for** over 3 months.
TRUE He was accused **of** stealing. We approved **of** her new boyfriend.	TRUE We're moving next year. (No Prep) He is **at** his computer surfing the net.
FALSE He was accused **about** stealing. We approved **with** her new boyfriend.	FALSE We're moving **in** next year. He is **by** his computer surfing the net.
TRUE I'd rather have wine instead **of** beer. We apologized **for** our loud music.	TRUE Jerry likes to read **on** the bus. Smoking **on** the plane is prohibited.
FALSE I'd rather have wine instead **to** beer. We apologized **about** our loud music.	FALSE Jerry likes to read **in** the bus. Smoking **in** the plane is prohibited.

Chapter 10. Guess My Occupation — Directions

OBJECTIVE:

To practice asking questions, get more familiar with verbs, sharpen listening comprehension skills, and expand work-related vocabulary.

HOW TO PREPARE FOR THIS LESSON:

Photocopy enough **Guess My Occupation** Study Sheets for each student and yourself.

Photocopy and cut out the **Guess My Occupation** Game Chips.

When you are ready to begin the lesson, scatter the strips of paper, face down, at the head of the table.

This game is basically a variation on 20 Questions, with which you already may be familiar.

Go over the study sheet as a class. The students can use this as a base for asking new questions not listed on the sheet.

NOW BEGIN:

Explain that an occupation is written on each strip of paper. One student sits at the head of the table, chooses a strip, and reads it quietly to himself/herself. It's not a bad idea to keep a dictionary at the head of the table so the student can look up the occupation for clarity.

**Save A Tree
Save Some Time**

Photocopy and cover both sides of the **Guess My Occupation** Game Chips sheets with clear packing tape before cutting them into pieces. This will make them more durable for repeated use.

Collect the game chips at the end of each lesson and place them in a labeled envelope for future use.

Chapter 10. Guess My Occupation — Directions

Page 116

Be flexible...

Be prepared for times when a simple "yes" or "no" doesn't adequately answer the question. Be a bit flexible; the occasional "maybe" or "sometimes," etc. may need to be used for the sake of a more accurate answer.

A Bright Idea !

You may want to take some time to talk about recent trends in removing gender distinctions from various job titles. For example, "waiters" and "waitresses" can now be called "servers." Instead of "mailman" or "mailwoman" we can now say "postal carrier."

When the student understands the occupation, the other students must ask only "yes" or "no" questions to try to figure out what is written on his/her strip of paper. The student who is able to guess first goes to the head of the class, chooses a new occupation, and begins the next round.

VARIATIONS:

As you may already be thinking, there are countless ways to alter this game to teach other specific question asking skills. Possible themes could be describing things found at work, household items, or famous companies. A sheet of Blank Game Chips are provided in the Appendix (page 248) should you want to custom-design a similar game.

Guess My Occupation — Study Sheet

Verbs

Does this person **wear** a uniform?
          help sick people?

Tools

Does this person carry a **gun**?
          use a **computer**?

Characteristics

Is this person **educated**?
        well-paid?

Description

Is this job **dangerous**?
      indoors?

Helpful Phrases

Is this person **in charge of...** ?
Is this person **responsible for...** ?

Does this person (usually) work **with** children?
                            in an office?
                            for someone else?

Page 118 Chapter 10. **Guess My Occupation** Game Chips #1

Secretary	Lawyer	Doctor
Nurse	Teacher	Veterinarian
Firefighter	Police Officer	Dentist
Postal Carrier	Plumber	Actor or Actress
Tailor	Soldier	Librarian
Farmer	Painter	Sailor
Cook	Waiter or Waitress	Barista
Politician	Mechanic	Pilot
Cab Driver	Truck Driver	Baker
Construction Worker	Optometrist	Maid

Chapter 10. **Guess My Occupation**   Game Chips #2

Engineer	Chef	Soccer Player
Robber / Thief	Street Performer	Janitor
Chiropractor	Clown	Carpenter
Bartender	Accountant	Architect
Librarian	Baker	Butcher
Photographer	Singer	Pharmacist
Pediatrician	Tour Guide	Chauffeur
Stock Broker	Realtor	Referee
Life Guard	Priest / Minister	Nun

Chapter 11. Name That Shop   Directions

OBJECTIVE:

To get the class familiar and comfortable with the vocabulary needed to describe common shops and government buildings in a town or city.

This is a good primer for the **Where Is The Post Office?** lesson.

HOW TO PREPARE FOR THIS LESSON:

Photocopy enough **Name That Shop** Worksheets and **Name That Shop** Answer Sheets for each student.

Photocopy one set of **Name That Shop** Game Chips sheets and cut them into their individual chips.

Divide the class into partners. If you have an odd number of students, make one group of three. Have them fill in their worksheets together.

After they have filled in as many as they can, go over the answers as a class. When everyone has filled in the correct answer for each question, give them 5-10 minutes to review these answers.

NOW BEGIN:

Divide the class into two teams. Have two students from one team sit at the front of the class. Place the

Page 121

A Bright Idea !

If you feel that, after doing the initial worksheets, your class may still have difficulty making the transition to describing places randomly on their own, be prepared with an additional copy of the worksheets with the answers filled in and cut into individual strips.

Have one half of the pair read from the strips and the partner try to guess the answer.

You can do this for points or just as a warm-up round for no points.

After a round of that, they should be better able to describe places in their own words.

Chapter 11. Name That Shop — Directions

Page 122

Cheater Alert !

Make sure that your students don't just shout out names of places rather than describing them. For example, if the phrase is "convenience store" and the student just shouts out names of well-known convenience stores (i.e. 7-11, Plaid Pantry, Casino, etc.), they haven't learned how to describe this place and their partner isn't developing their listening comprehension skills.

Make it clear from the beginning that if they use proper nouns to describe a shop or store, they will forfeit that point.

game chips, face down, near the two players.

Player A chooses a chip and has to describe the shop written on it without using any part of the shop title in their explanation. Player B has to try to guess as many of the shops as possible within a certain amount of time (30-45 seconds depending on the level of the class). Each correct answer earns their team a point. When the round is over, the current players return to their seats, two new players from the opposing team go to the front of the class, and a new round begins.

The team with the most points at the end of the game wins.

You may choose to go through all the shops only once or recycle used game chips back into the pile. If you choose to use the game chips only once, the game ends when there are no more chips. If you choose to recycle the used game chips, the game ends when you feel that the students have learned the vocabulary or start to lose interest in the game.

Name That Shop   Worksheet #1

1. This is a place where people like to go to relax. This is a nice place to walk your dog, have a picnic, feed the birds, or play Frisbee. Usually, there are lots of trees around.

    (Answer)_____

2. This is a quiet place that people go to when they want to read or borrow books, videos, or music CDs. Students sometimes go here to study or do research.

    (Answer)_____

3. This is where men go to get their hair cut.

    (Answer)_____

4. This is where people go to buy bread and pastries.

    (Answer)_____

5. This is where people go to mail letters or receive packages. You can also buy postage stamps and package materials here.

    (Answer)_____

6. This is a dark place where people can go to watch movies and eat fresh popcorn.

    (Answer)_____

7. This is where people can buy used or second hand items like clothes, shoes, or household items. The prices are low and the products are usually in pretty good condition.

    (Answer)_____

8. This is where people go when they need to take care of their teeth.

    (Answer)_____

9. This is where people go when they are very sick and need to see a doctor.

    (Answer)_____

Name That Shop   Worksheet #2

10. This is a government building that's responsible for keeping the neighborhood safe from crime.

    (Answer)_____

11. This type of restaurant is for people who don't eat meat.

    (Answer)_____

12. At this type of restaurant you can order pasta, garlic bread, and pizza.

    (Answer)_____

13. At this type of restaurant you can get burritos, tacos, and enchiladas.

    (Answer)_____

14. At this type of restaurant you can buy egg rolls, fried rice, and fortune cookies.

    (Answer)_____

15. This is a place where women can go to get their hair cut and styled.

    (Answer)_____

16. If you need tools and supplies for building something, you might go here.

    (Answer)_____

17. If you need to buy supplies for sewing, knitting, or crocheting, you could go to this place.

    (Answer)_____

18. This is a place for women to buy fashionable clothes, shoes, and accessories. The items in such stores are often expensive.

    (Answer)_____

19. This is where people go to gamble. You can usually find slot machines and card tables here.

    (Answer)_____

Name That Shop   Worksheet #3

20. This is where busy parents sometimes take their young kids. Sometimes a company provides this for their employees' children and sometimes parents have to pay a service to look after their kids.

   (Answer)_____

21. This is where people pay to get exercise. Most of these places have free weights, exercise equipment, various exercise classes, and a pool.

   (Answer)_____

22. This is where you can buy games, dolls, and sports equipment for children.

   (Answer)_____

23. At this store you can buy various alcoholic beverages like wine, beer, or hard spirits.

   (Answer)_____

24. This is where friends go to listen to music, dance, and usually drink.

   (Answer)_____

25. This can be indoors or outdoors. This is a place to watch professional soccer or baseball games.

   (Answer)_____

26. This place provides medical care for animals. This is where you'd take a sick pet.

   (Answer)_____

27. This is where you can look at paintings, drawings, or sculptures. Children sometimes go here for school field trips.

   (Answer)_____

28. This is a building of worship for Jewish people.

   (Answer)_____

29. This is a building of worship for Christians and Catholics.

   (Answer)_____

FUN, QUICK & EASY   Game-Based Activities for Teachers of Adult ESL

Name That Shop   Worksheet #4

30. This is a building of worship for Muslim people.

    (Answer)_____

31. This is a large building that contains a variety of shops, stores, and restaurants inside.

    (Answer)_____

32. This is a place to buy earrings, necklaces, or bracelets. You can usually get your watch repaired here.

    (Answer)_____

33. This is where people open accounts, deposit their money, and cash checks. If people need help with their accounts or have any questions, there are tellers there to help them.

    (Answer)_____

34. This is where old people go to meet other old people. There are usually activities and classes available here specifically for old or retired people.

    (Answer)_____

35. This is where dead people are taken to be prepared for burial.

    (Answer)_____

36. This place sells a little of everything but mostly it sells snack food. You can also buy cigarettes, magazines, beer, motor oil, and lottery tickets. This place is usually smaller than a supermarket and the prices are a little higher, but they have many more locations and are more common to find.

    (Answer)_____

37. This place sells things like tables, chairs, bureaus, and beds. Some sell home or office accessories as well, like lamps or rugs.

    (Answer)_____

38. This is where little kids go to learn how to read and write and do math. The kids that go to this place are too old for kindergarten.

    (Answer)_____

Name That Shop — Answer Sheet

Use the words below to fill in the blanks.

Art Museum	Fabric Store	Movie Theater
Bakery	Fitness Club	Park
Bank	Funeral Parlor	Police Station
Barber Shop	Furniture Store	Post Office
Boutique	Hair Salon	Senior Center
Casino	Hardware Store	Shopping Mall
Chinese Restaurant	Hospital	Sports Arena
Church	Italian Restaurant	Synagogue
Convenience Store	Jewelry Store	Thrift Store
Daycare Center	Library	Toy Store
Dentist	Liquor Store	Vegetarian Restaurant
Disco	Mexican Restaurant	Veterinarian
Elementary School	Mosque	

(fold)

Answer Key

1. Park
2. Library
3. Barber Shop
4. Bakery
5. Post Office
6. Movie Theater
7. Thrift Store
8. Dentist
9. Hospital
10. Police Station
11. Vegetarian Restaurant
12. Italian Restaurant
13. Mexican Restaurant
14. Chinese Restaurant
15. Hair Salon
16. Hardware Store
17. Fabric Store
18. Boutique
19. Casino
20. Daycare Center
21. Fitness Club
22. Toy Store
23. Liquor Store
24. Disco
25. Sports Arena
26. Veterinarian
27. Art Museum
28. Synagogue
29. Church
30. Mosque
31. Shopping Mall
32. Jewelry Store
33. Bank
34. Senior Center
35. Funeral Parlor
36. Convenience Store
37. Furniture Store
38. Elementary School

Page 128 — Chapter 11. **Name That Shop** — Game Chips #1

SUPERMARKET	FLOWER SHOP	VEGETARIAN RESTAURANT
BUTCHER SHOP	HIGH SCHOOL	POLICE STATION
MOVIE THEATER	ELEMENTARY SCHOOL	ITALIAN RESTAURANT
BAKERY	COLLEGE / UNIVERSITY	CASINO
HARDWARE STORE	POST OFFICE	HOSPITAL
THRIFT STORE	FIRE STATION	GAS STATION
BOUTIQUE	BEAUTY PARLOR	COFFEE SHOP
BARBERSHOP	CITY HALL	DENTIST
BAR / PUB	LIBRARY	BANK
DAYCARE CENTER	CHINESE RESTAURANT	SENIOR CENTER

Chapter 11. **Name That Shop** Game Chips #2

BUS STATION	SUBWAY STATION	AIRPORT
PHARMACY	PIZZA PARLOR	COMMUNITY CENTER
CONCERT HALL	SPORTS STADIUM	JEWELRY STORE
FURNITURE STORE	APARTMENT BUILDING	ART GALLERY
MUSEUM	SHOPPING MALL	POOL
FUNERAL PARLOR	CEMETARY / GRAVEYARD	AMUSEMENT PARK
RACE TRACK	SKI / ROLLER RINK	TENNIS COURT
FITNESS CLUB	PLAYGROUND	NURSERY SCHOOL
NIGHT CLUB	ICE CREAM PARLOR	DONUT SHOP
TRAIN STATION	CANDY SHOP / STORE	DISCO

BOOKSTORE	MARKET	TOY STORE
MUSIC STORE	ELECTRONICS STORE	CONVENIENCE STORE
LIQUOR STORE	CHURCH	MOSQUE
BUS STOP	SYNAGOGUE	TEMPLE
SHRINE	PARK	BIKE SHOP
AUTO / CAR DEALERSHIP	CLOTHES STORE	FABRIC STORE
VETERINARIAN	PEDIATRICIAN	KINDERGARTEN

Chapter 12. **Where's the Post Office?** Directions

OBJECTIVE:

To teach students how to ask for, understand, and give clear directions.

HOW TO PREPARE FOR THIS LESSON:

Photocopy enough **Where's the Post Office?** Study Sheets for each student and yourself.

Photocopy one set of **Where's the Post Office?** Maps and photocopy and cut out one sheet of **Where's the Post Office?** Game Chips for each set of partners.

Go over the study sheet as a class.

NOW BEGIN:

This is partner work.

Student A has a street map with all the buildings shown on it. Student B has the same map but with most of the buildings missing. Without being able to see each other's map, Student B places the game chips on his/her incomplete map based on Student A's directions.

Student B should be encouraged to ask for clarifying information if he/she is unclear about any of the directions.

Page 131

Prior to this Lesson:

Depending on the level of your students, it might be best to complete:

- Architect

- Name That Shop

prior to doing this lesson.

**Save A Tree
Save Some Time**

Photocopy and cover both sides of your **Where's the Post Office?** Game Chips sheets with clear packing tape before cutting them into pieces. This will make them more durable for repeated use.

Collect the game chips at the end of each lesson and place them in a labeled envelope for future use.

Chapter 12. Where's the Post Office? Directions

Page 132

A Bright Idea !

If you have extra time at the end of the lesson, ask the students to give directions from, for example, a nearby bus stop or coffee shop to class.

If you're teaching in a large school building, have the students use the same language they've just learned to explain what classrooms are where in your building.

At the end of the round, Student A and Student B compare their maps to see if they match.

Hand out Map #2 and Map #2 Answer and have the students reverse roles so that Student B gives directions and Student A places the shops on the incomplete map.

It's best to start with Map #1, the easiest, and work your way up to Map #6.

Where's the Post Office?   Study Sheet

North
West + East
South

The Florist is **on the southwest corner of** *Main and 1st.*

Mr Brown lives **around the corner from** *the Bakery.*

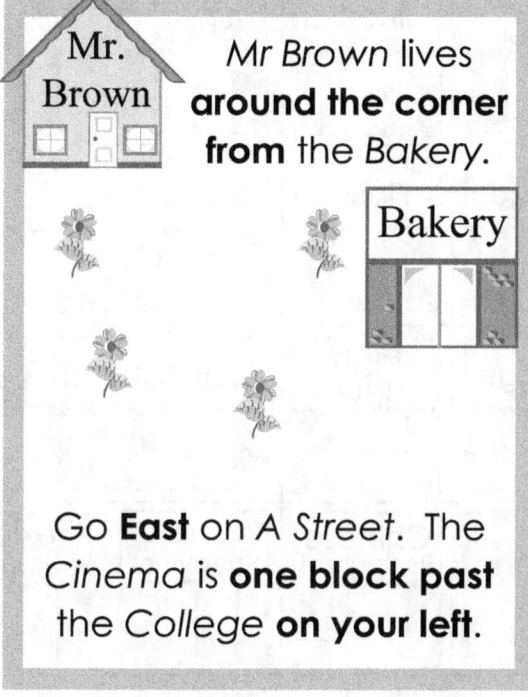

Go **East** *on A Street. The Cinema is* **one block past** *the College* **on your left.**

A Street

Ms. Green's house is **next to** *the Hospital.*

The Dentist is **across the street from** *the Market.*

The High School is **between** *the Market and the Fire Department.*

The Market is **on the corner of** *1st Avenue and A Street.*

FUN, QUICK & EASY   Game-Based Activities for Teachers of Adult ESL

Page 134 — Chapter 12. **Where's the Post Office?** Game Chips

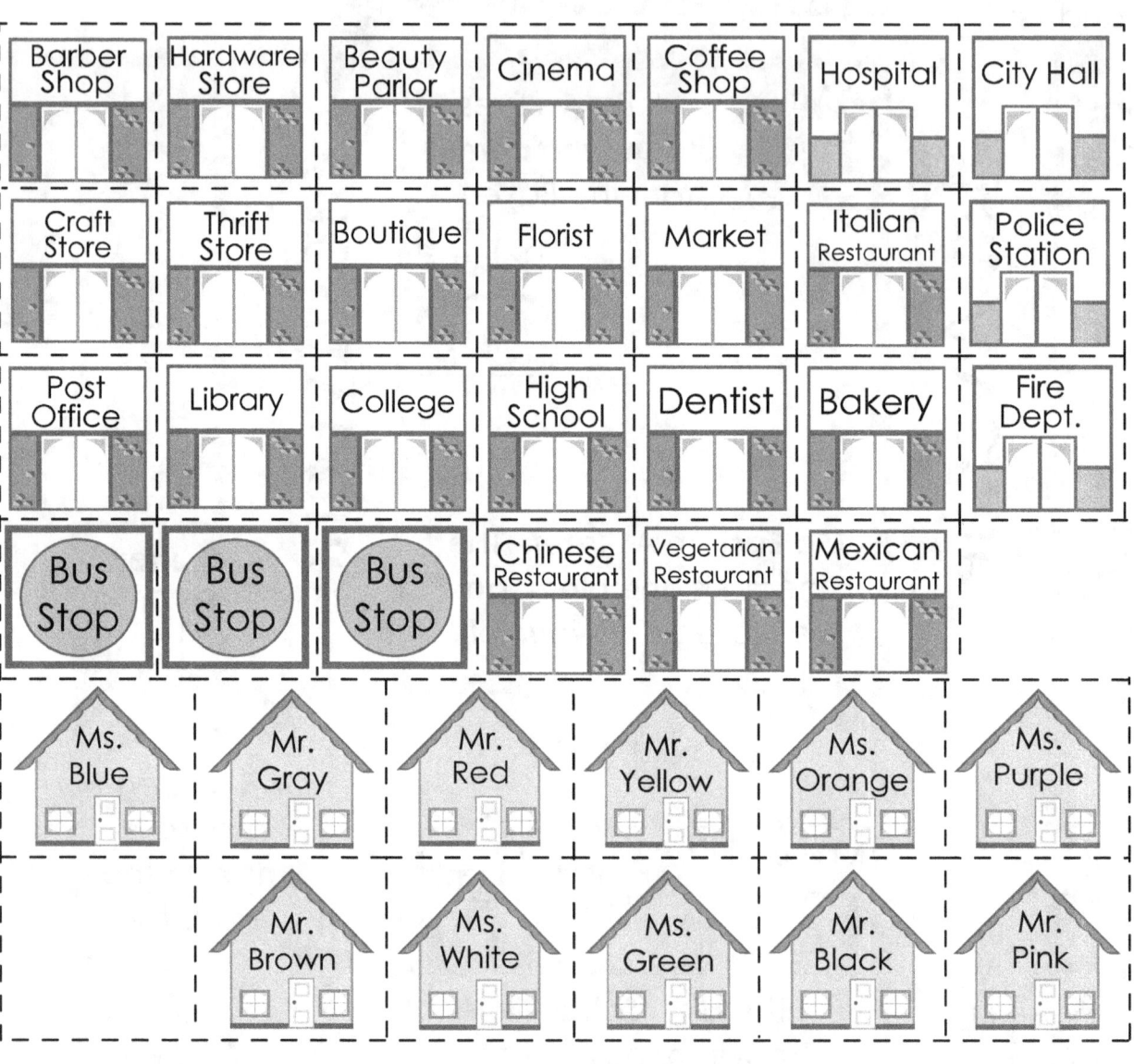

Where's the Post Office?   Map #1   Answer

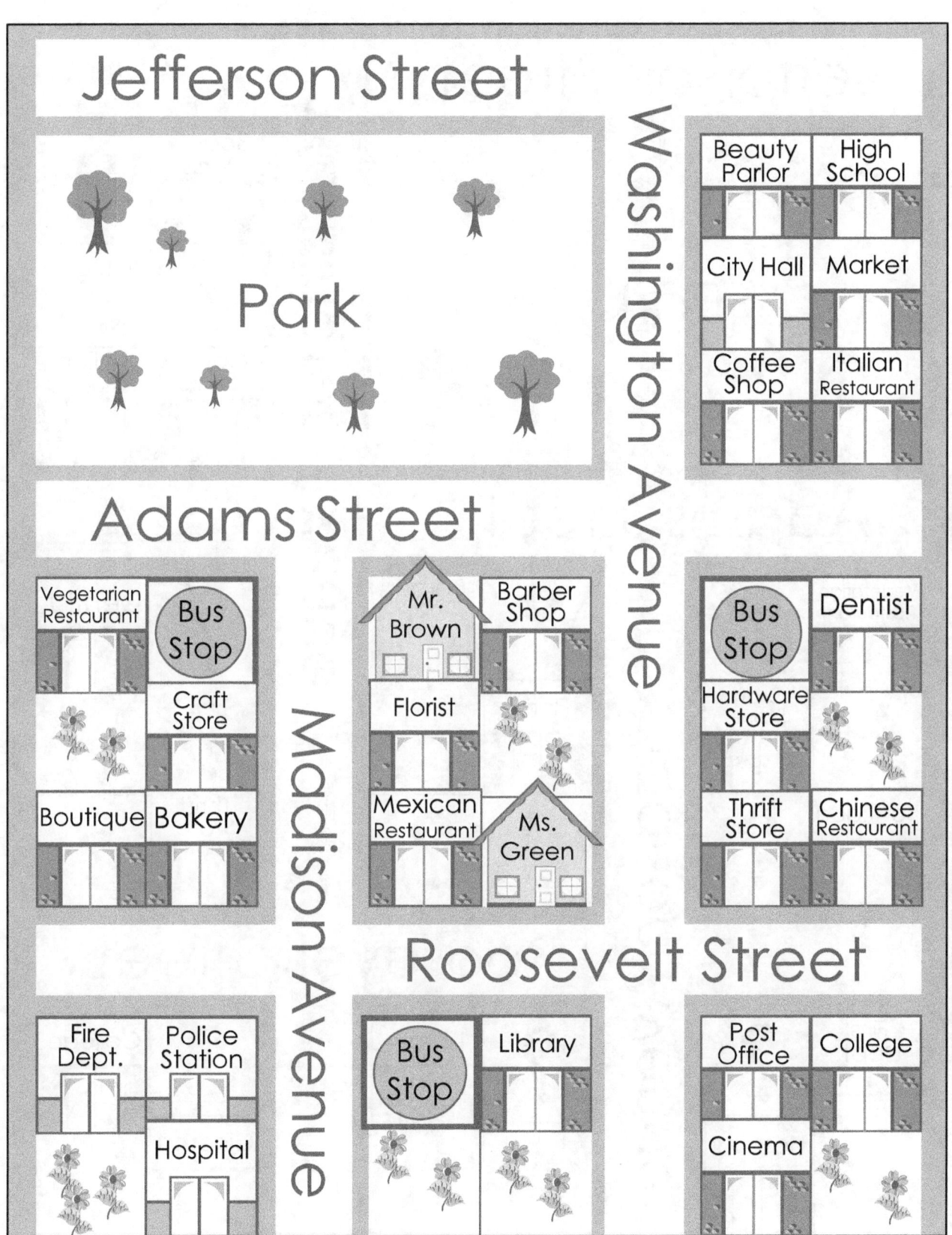

Where's the Post Office? Map #1

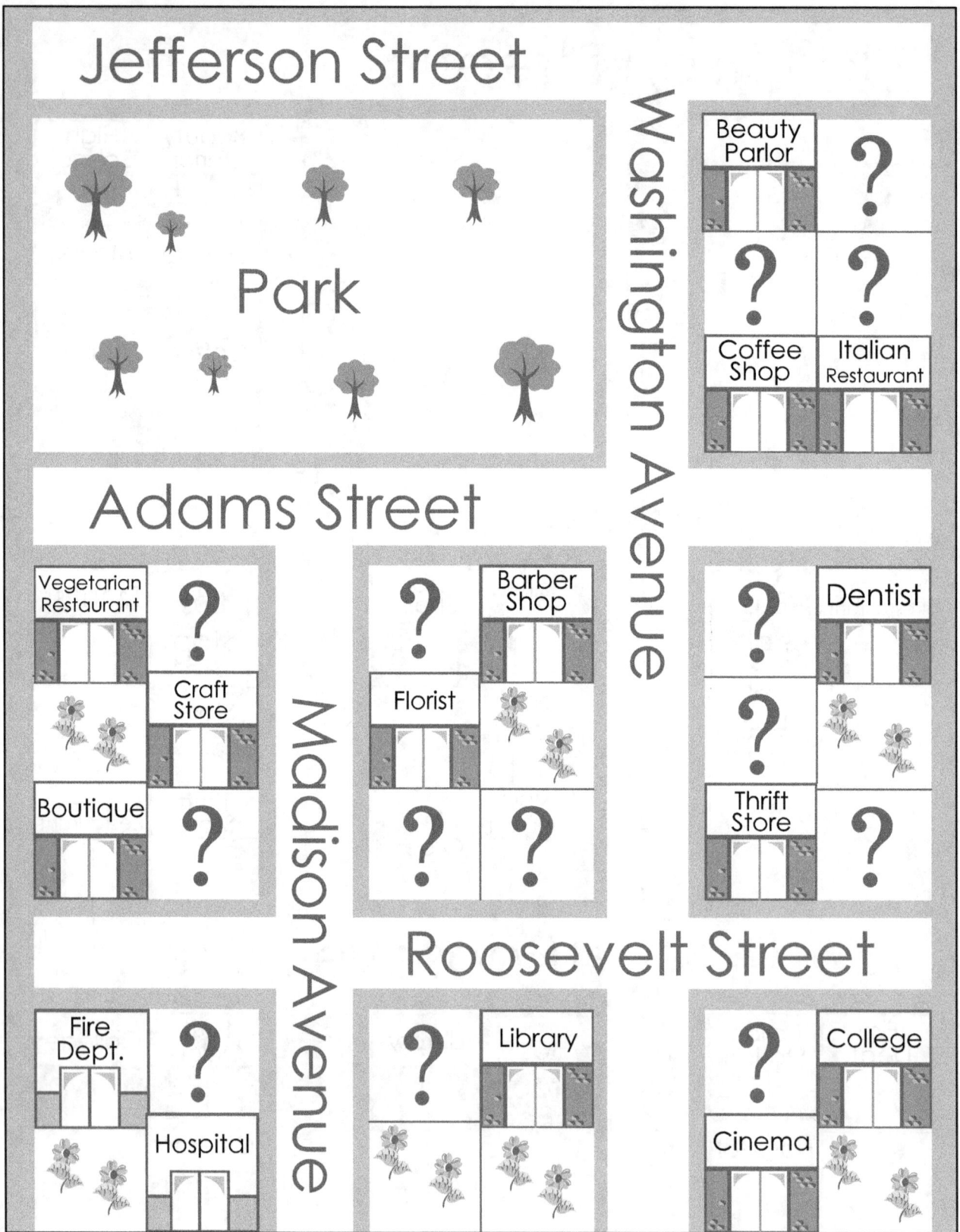

Page 136 FUN, QUICK & EASY Game-Based Activities for Teachers of Adult ESL

Where's the Post Office?   Map #2   Answer

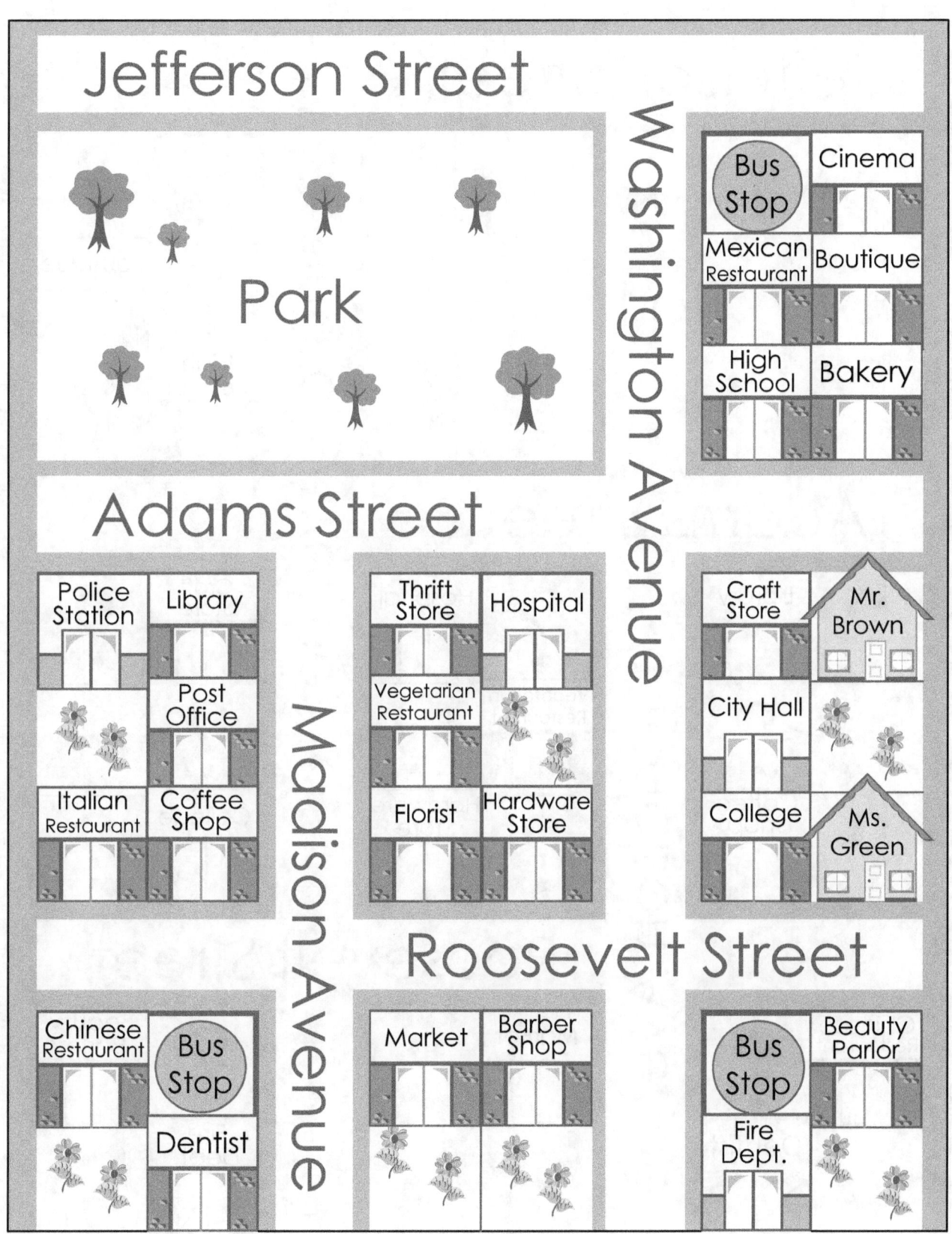

Fun, Quick & Easy   Game-Based Activities for Teachers of Adult ESL

Where's the Post Office?   Map #2

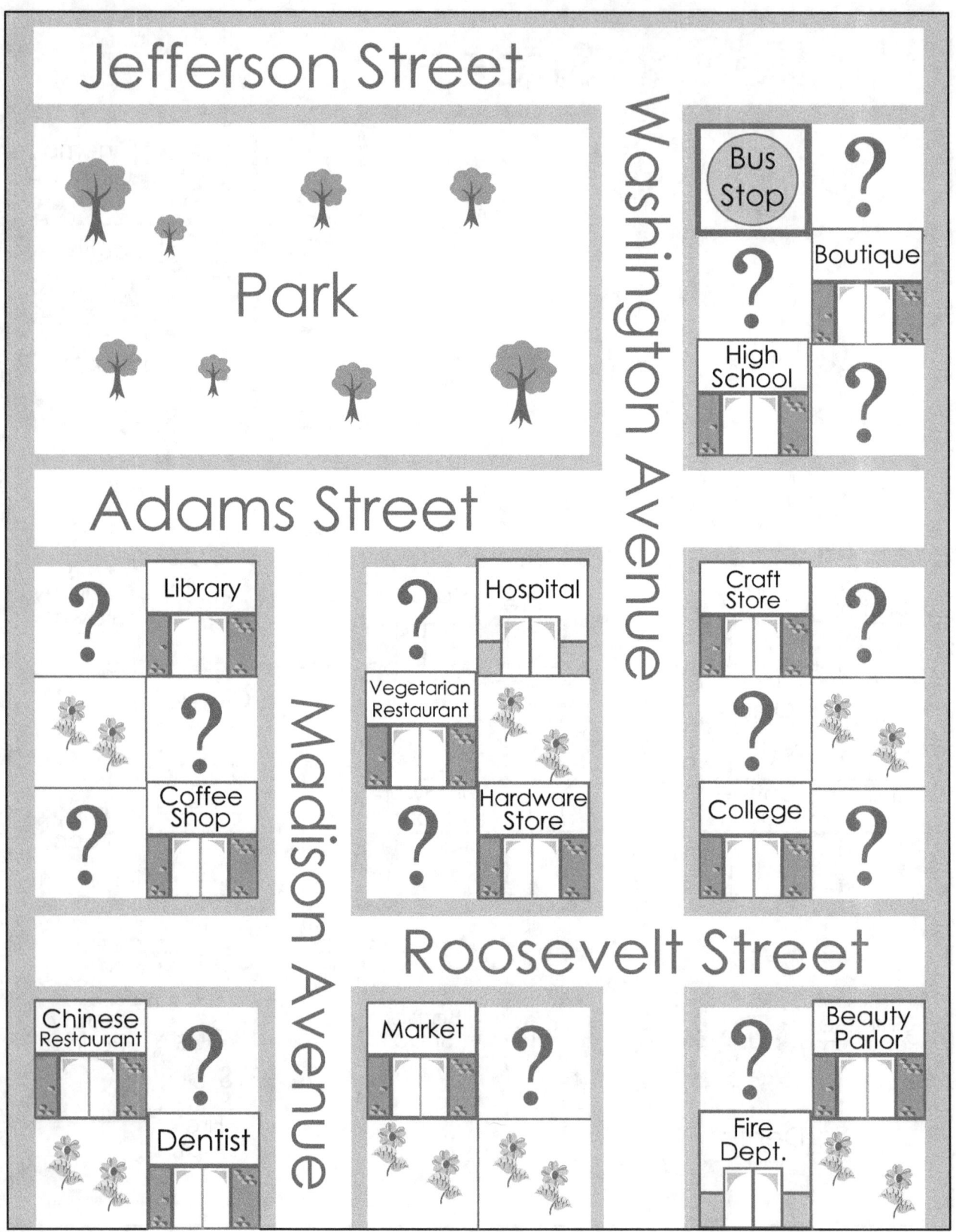

Page 138   FUN, QUICK & EASY   Game-Based Activities for Teachers of Adult ESL

Where's the Post Office? Map #3 Answer

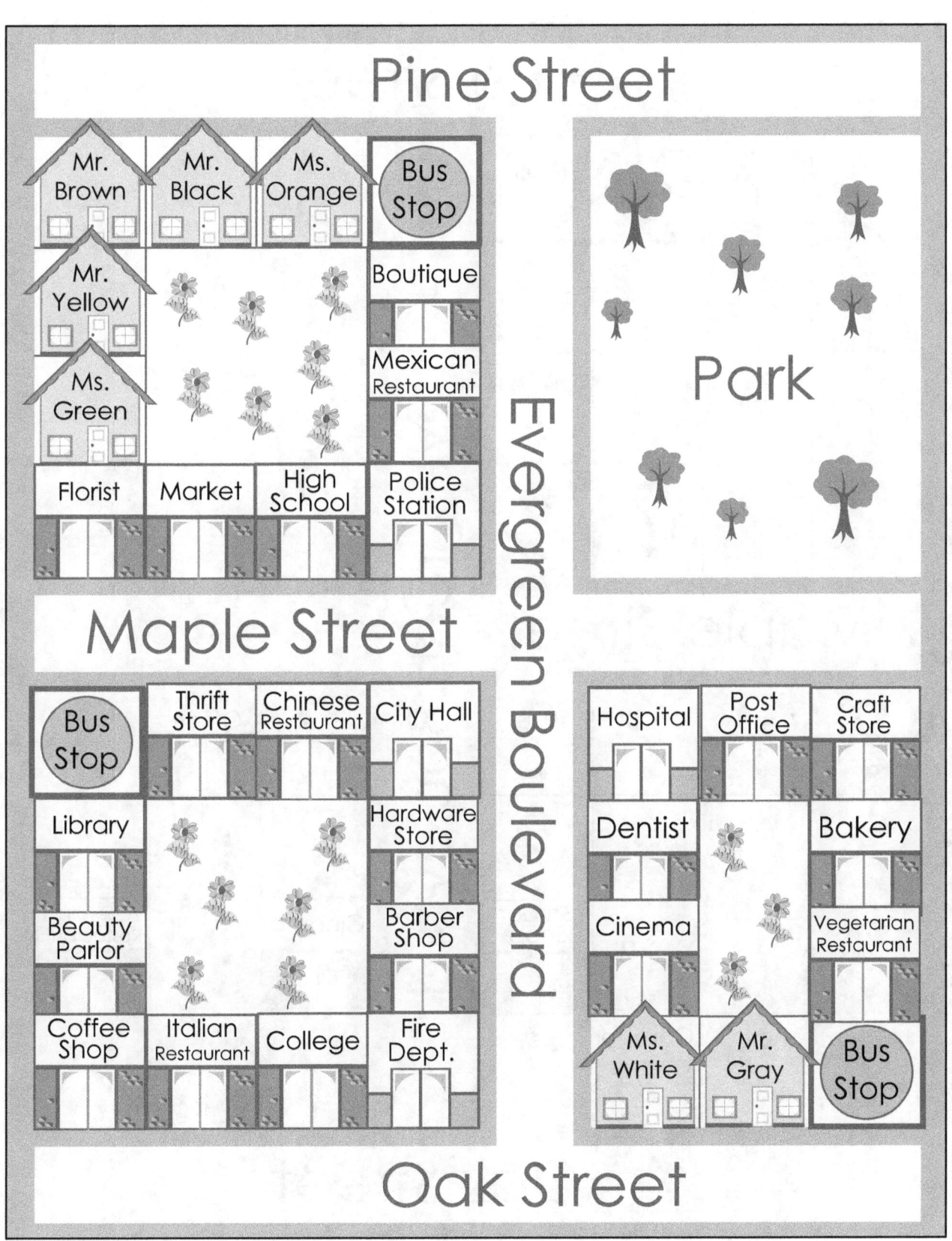

Where's the Post Office? Map #3

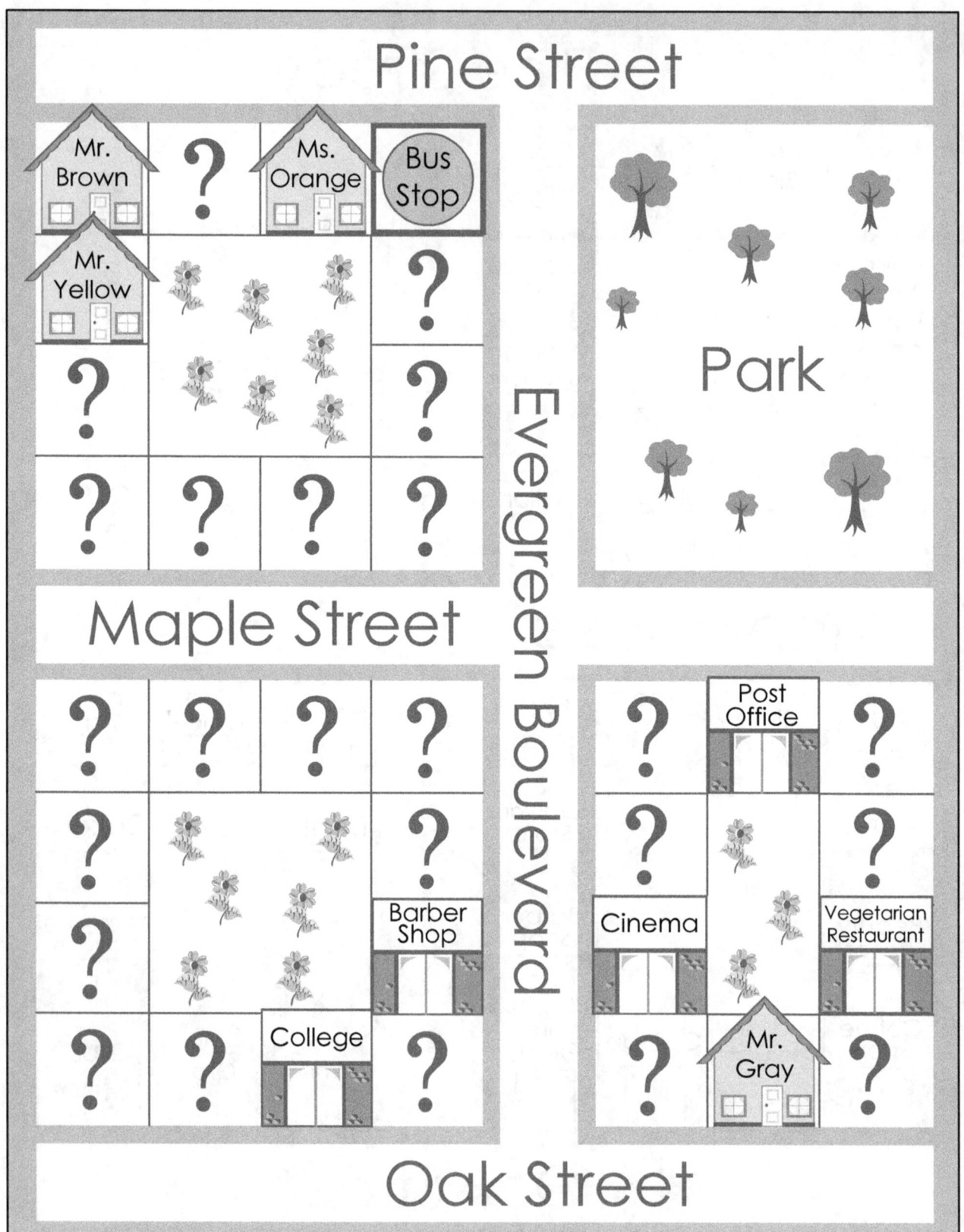

Page 140   **FUN, QUICK & EASY**   Game-Based Activities for Teachers of Adult ESL

Where's the Post Office? Map #4 Answer

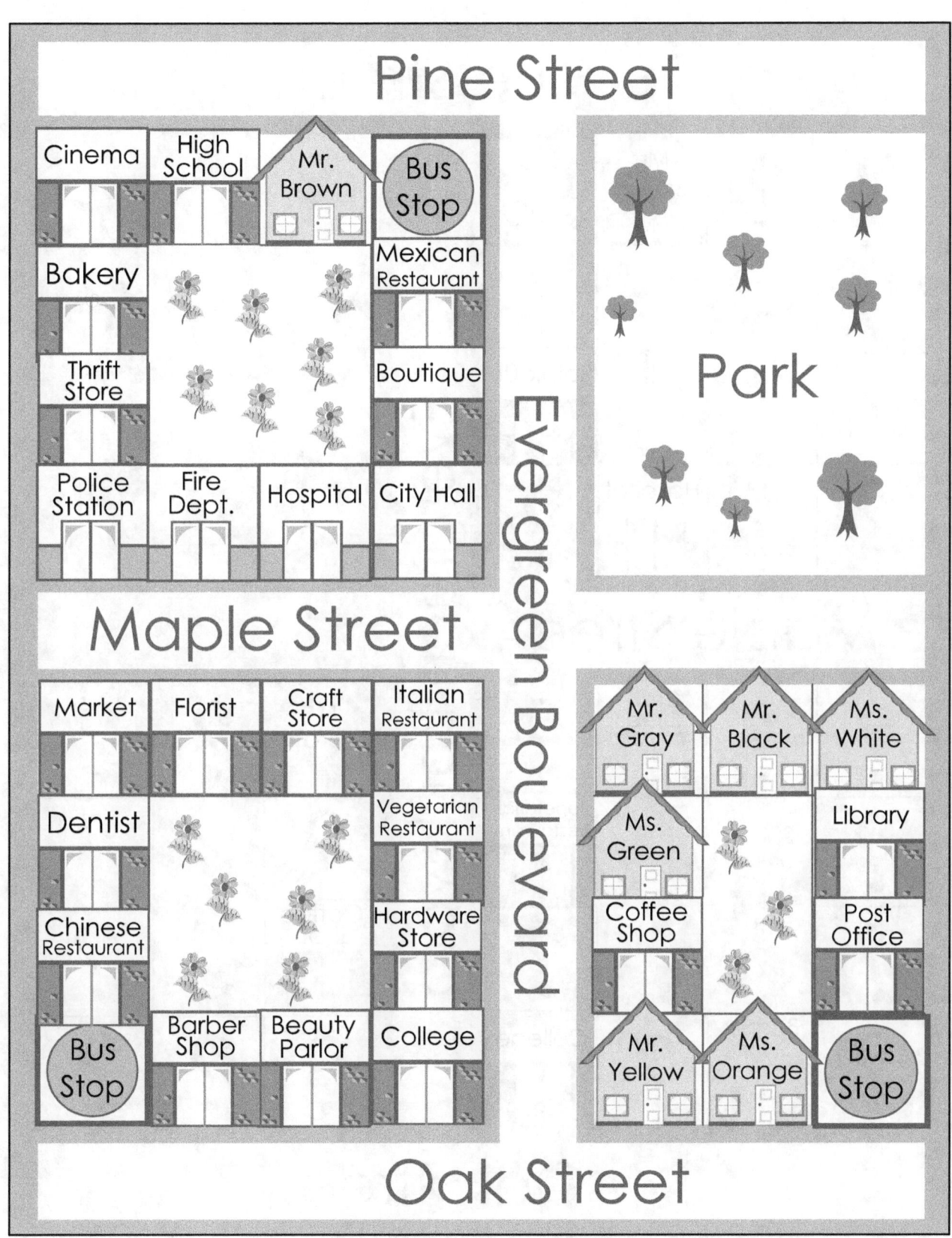

Where's the Post Office?   Map #4

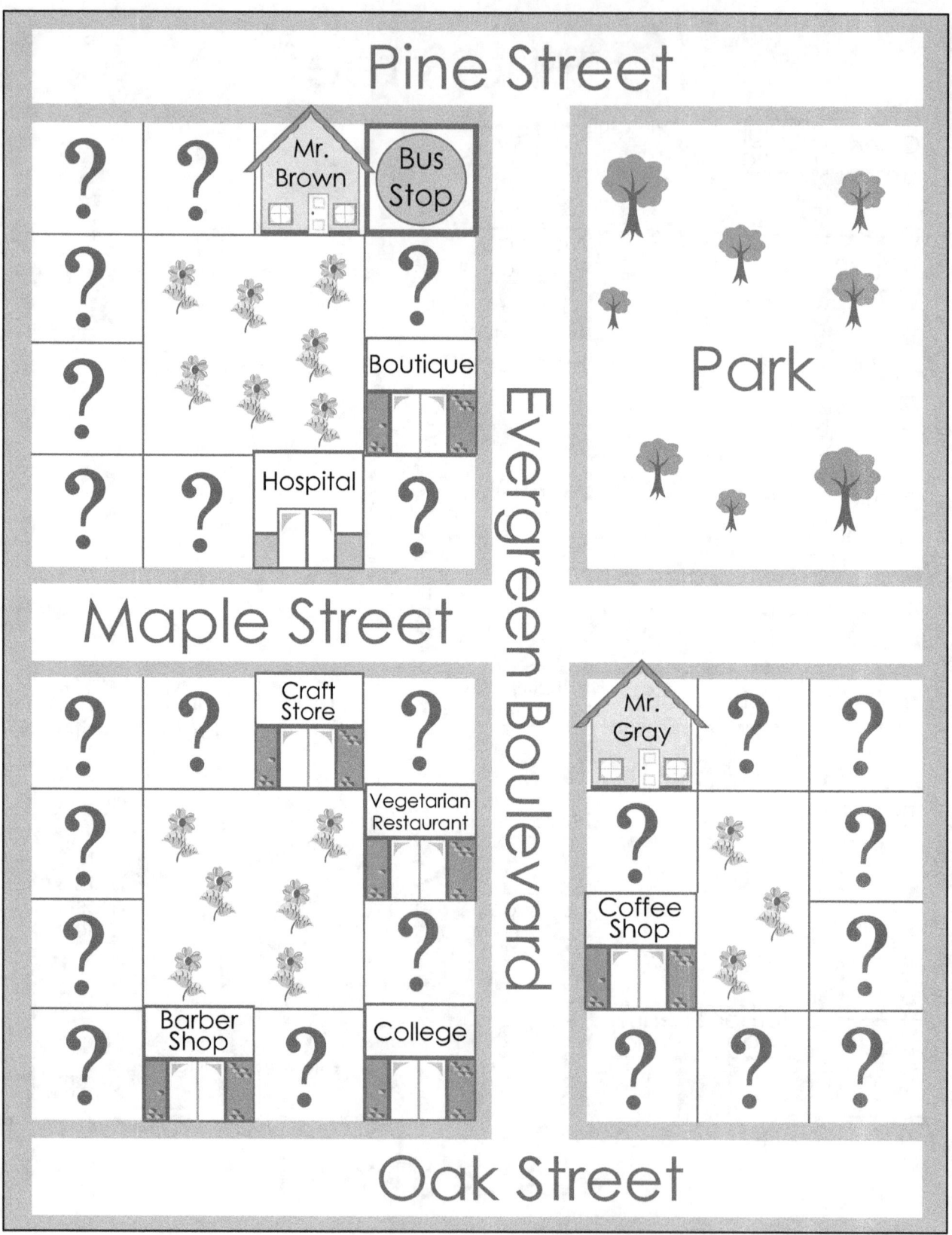

Where's the Post Office? Map #5 Answer

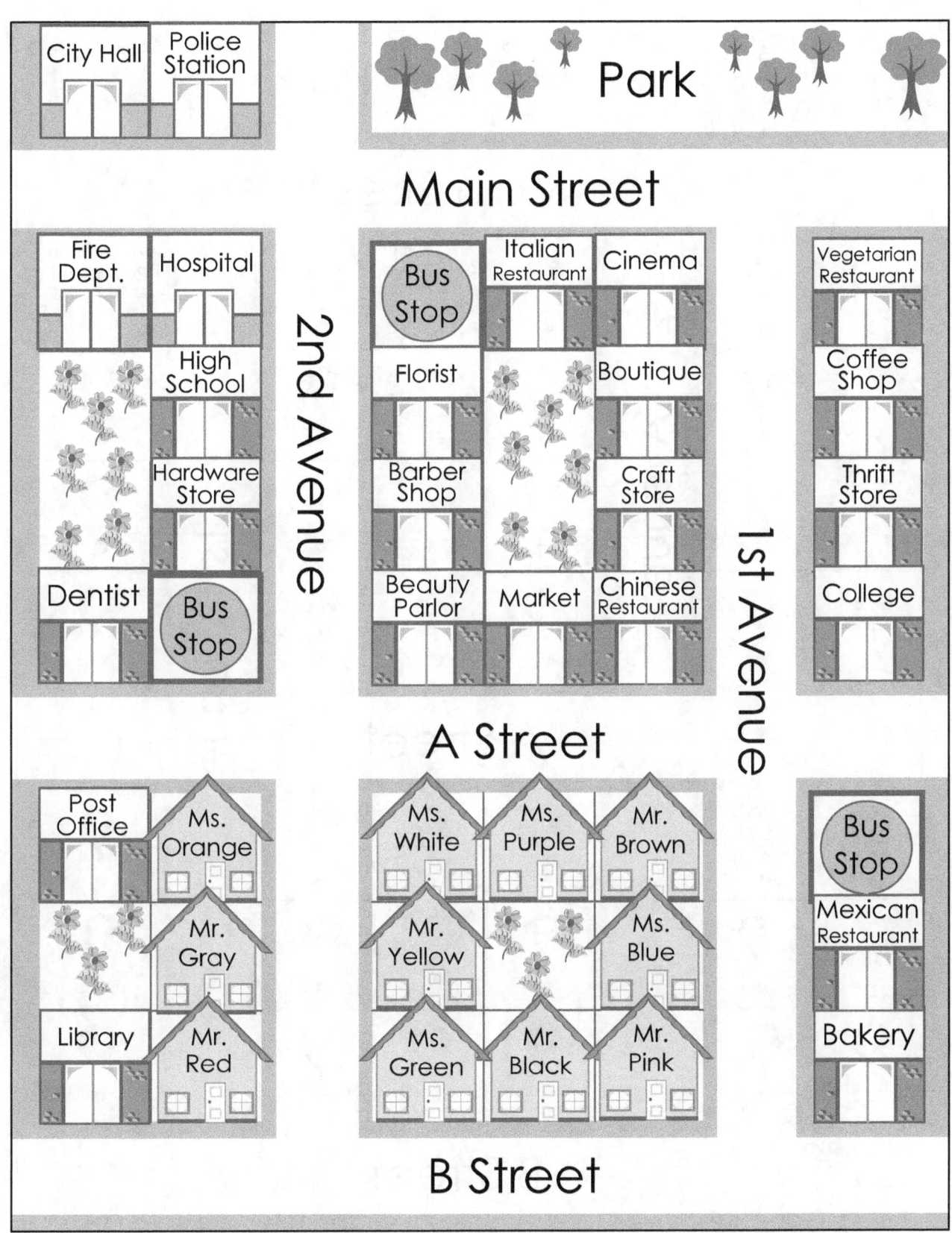

Where's the Post Office?   Map #5

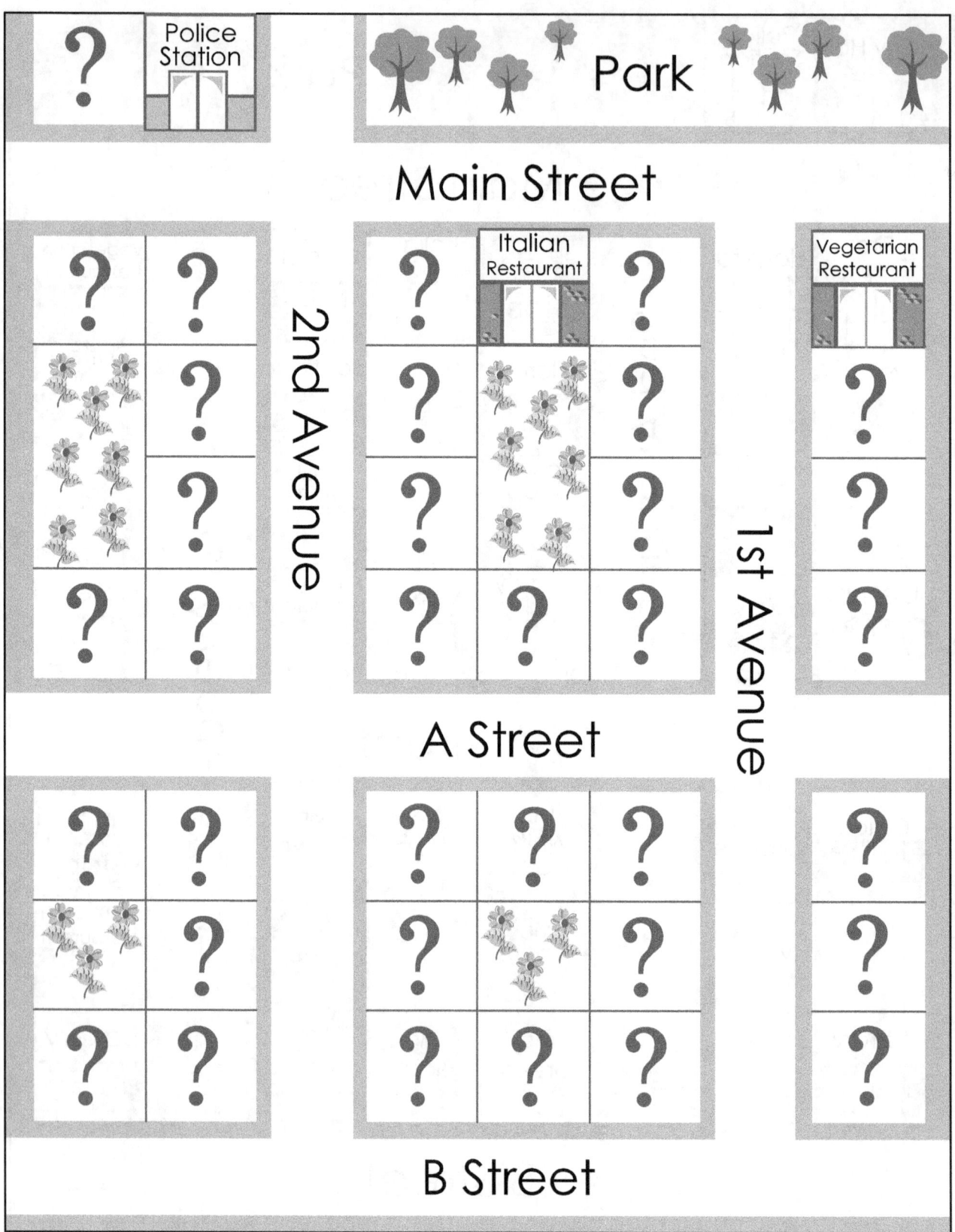

Page 144   FUN, QUICK & EASY   Game-Based Activities for Teachers of Adult ESL

Where's the Post Office? Map #6 Answer

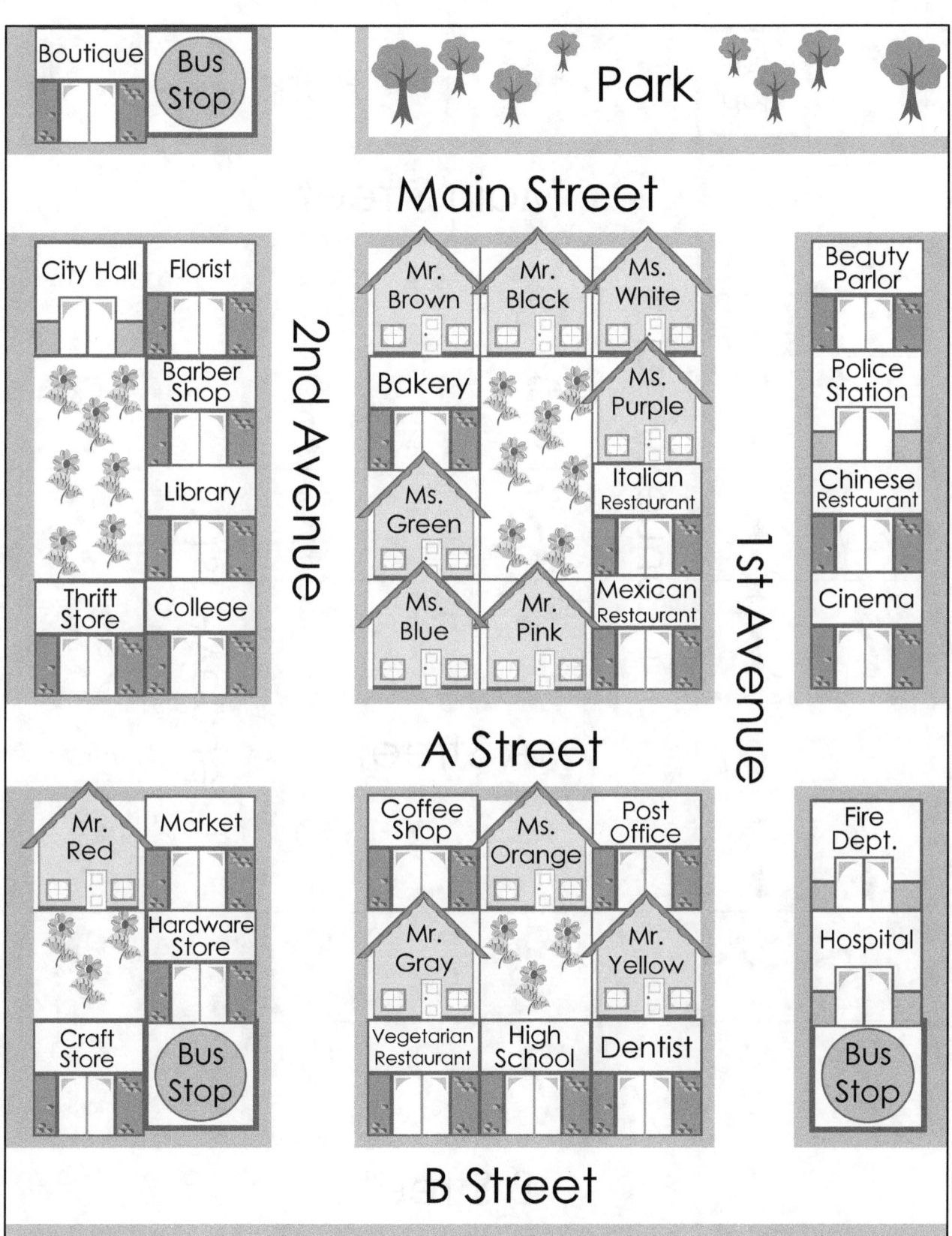

Fun, Quick & Easy   Game-Based Activities for Teachers of Adult ESL

Where's the Post Office?   Map #6

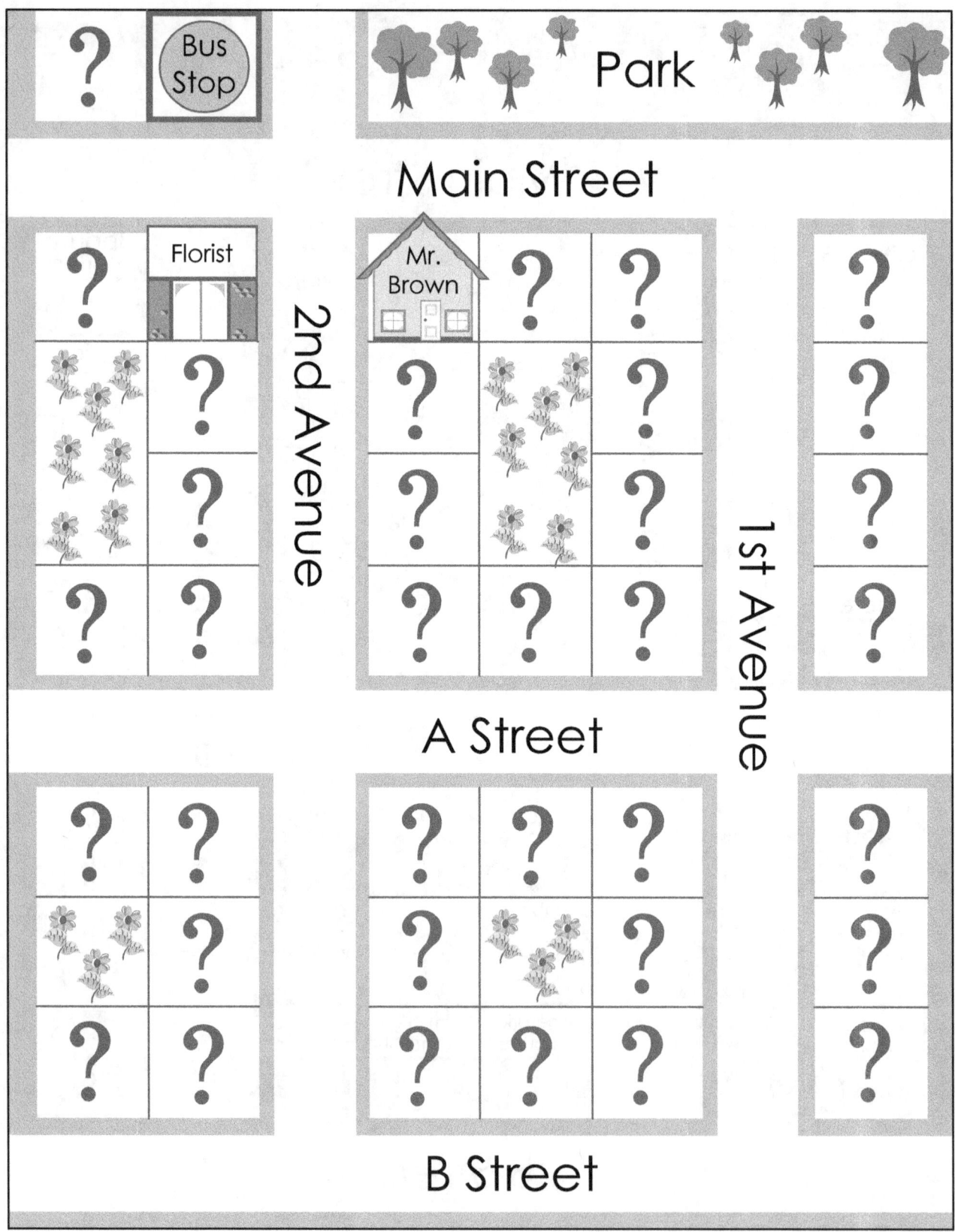

Page 146   FUN, QUICK & EASY   Game-Based Activities for Teachers of Adult ESL

Chapter 13. Hangman for Small Talk — Directions

OBJECTIVE:

To introduce common questions and answers used in basic small talk.

HOW TO PREPARE FOR THIS LESSON:

Prepare a list of twenty sentences: ten questions and their corresponding answers. Here's a sample, but you certainly don't have to use it:

1. What's your name?
2. My name is Bond. James Bond.
3. Where are you from?
4. I'm from London, England.
5. What do you do?
6. I'm an international spy.
7. Are you married?
8. Heavens no. I'm single.
9. Do you have any children?
10. None that I know of.
11. Do you have any brothers or sisters?
12. I am an only child.
13. Who do you work for?
14. I work for Her Majesty's Secret Service.
15. Is this your first time in Paris?
16. No, I visit Paris regularly.
17. How do you like Paris?
18. It's a lovely city.
19. What are your hobbies?
20. I enjoy chasing women and drinking dry martinis.

A Bright Idea !

If you think this lesson is too ambitious for your class, then start with single words instead—just like in the typical way Hangman is played. It might help if there is a theme to the words, such as "household items" or "things found in an office."

If you're teaching an absolute beginner's class, Hangman is a good way to get students more familiar with the alphabet. The **Alphabet Hot Potato** lesson (page 17) might be a good precursor to this lesson.

Chapter 13. Hangman for Small Talk — Directions

A Bright Idea !

You can use this lesson format for other exchanges, such as calling a customer or taking a message.

You might balk at the idea of expecting students to be able to memorize 20 sentences at a time. Rest assured, I have used this lesson many times and they always manage to do it because:

- There is a theme.

- There is a Question & Answer format, which provides additional structure.

If you adhere to these two guidelines, that should make it easier for your students.

NOW BEGIN:

Divide the class into two teams or have everyone play for themselves. On the board, clearly make enough blank spaces for each letter in sentence #1.

Include all required punctuation. For example:

1. _ _ _ _'_ / _ _ _ _ / _ _ _ _ ?   (for "What's your name?")

Go around the room asking each student to guess a letter. If the letter is in the sentence, fill it in. If not, write it at the bottom of the board. After someone has correctly guessed this sentence, fill in any missing letters and go around the class having each student read it. Erase sentence #1 and put up the blanks for sentence #2.

After someone has correctly guessed sentence #2, fill in any missing letters and go around the class having each student read it. After each student has read sentence #2, say "Sentence one," indicating that the next student should repeat the first sentence "What is your name?" Then say "Sentence two," indicating that the next student should answer "My name is Bond. James Bond."

When everyone is comfortable with asking for and giving their name, move on to sentence #3 and so on.

Chapter 13. **Hangman for Small Talk**   Directions

As the sentences increase, it will become more challenging to keep them all straight but since there is a theme—small talk—this shouldn't be too difficult. However, it's not a bad idea to keep your list of sentences with you at all times in case you get confused.

Go through all 20 sentences until everyone is fairly comfortable reciting the correct sentence depending on what number you call out.

Now, erase the board completely and have two students go to the front of the class. Explain that they are at a party and are meeting for the first time. They can use their own names and information or new names but they cannot be James Bond anymore. They are to shake hands and let the small talk begin. Go around the class until each student has had a turn.

Caution !

Depending on the nationality of your students, you may want to go over how to shake hands when meeting someone for the first time.

This seemingly minor act can cause all sorts of discomfort for those not used to such a greeting. There may also be issues regarding men and women touching each other's hands.

Try to be culturally sensitive when necessary but also make it clear that this is a common practice in most Western cultures and that the refusal to shake another person's hand could be considered impolite, if not openly hostile.

Chapter 14. **Drawn to Homonyms**   Directions

Page 151

OBJECTIVE:

To expand basic vocabulary and to clear up some confusion when it comes to homonyms—words that sound alike but are spelled differently and have different meanings.

HOW TO PREPARE FOR THIS LESSON:

A week before class, tell your students that if they don't have a bilingual dictionary yet they should get one soon because they will need it for next week's lesson.

Prior to class, think about how many groups of students you would have if you divided the class into groups of 3-4. Make enough copies of the homonyms list—one for each group. Cut the sheets into their individual homonyms. The trick will be to keep the individual groups of cut out homonyms separated and in order. You'll also want an ample supply of scratch paper.

NOW BEGIN:

Have the students separate into groups of 3 or 4. There should be a table or desk for each group to draw on and at least one dictionary per group. It's not a bad idea to bring a spare dictionary just in case. Hand out a small stack of scratch paper to each group.

Note:

The homonyms list is rather long. Don't feel obliged to use every single word for this lesson—it would take much longer than a 2 hour class to accomplish that. Simply pick the ones you like best.

A Bright Idea !

You may want to reserve some time at the end of class and have students give sentences using the new vocabulary they've learned.

Save A Tree

You can use discarded paper from the paper recycling bins for students to draw on. As long as one side is clean and the paper is not too wrinkled, this should work fine.

Chapter 14. **Drawn to Homonyms**   Directions

Page 152

A Bright Idea !

If you're teaching a class where all the students speak the same language, try to learn some of their homonyms and the English equivalents. You can use the **Blank Game Chips** sheet in the Appendix (page 248) to create your variation on this lesson.

Don't tell the students the lesson is based on homonyms. At the end of the lesson, see if anyone can figure out that they learned the English words for some of their homonyms. Make sure everyone knows what a homonym is.

If there's time, ask your students if they can tell you any other homonyms in their language and what the English words for them would be.

Assign a Sketcher to each group. Hand out the first word to each Sketcher. They are not to show this word to anyone. If they don't know what this word means, they may look it up in their dictionary. When each Sketcher understands the word and pencils/pens are in hand, say "Go" (or something like that).

The Sketcher is to wordlessly and without additional gestures—this is not charades, after all—try to draw the word for his/her teammates to try to guess. The first team to guess the word correctly earns a point. When the first round is complete, hand a new word to the next Sketcher and start again.

VARIATIONS:

Obviously, this lesson is extremely flexible and can be used for any number of vocabulary lessons. A Blank Game Chips sheet is included in the Appendix (page 248) should you decide to custom-design your own lesson.

One thought is to build the lesson around a theme, for example "Vacations." See which team can figure out the theme first, based on the vocabulary learned.

bury	berry	base
bass	beat	beet
blew	blue	bored
board	buy	bye
cell	sell	chews
choose	flower	flour
chilly	chili	die
dye	ferry	fairy
fir	fur	flea
flee	flew	flu

Chapter 14. **Drawn to Homonyms** Game Chips #3

hair	hare	heal
heel	herd	heard
higher	hire	leek
leak	mail	male
maize	maze	moose
mousse	muscle	mussel
naval	navel	one
won	pain	pane
pair	pear	pea
pee	poor	pour

Chapter 14. **Drawn to Homonyms**   Game Chips #4

prophet	profit	quartz
quarts	rain	rein
right	write	ring
wring	root	route
sea	see	son
sun	sole	soul
soar	sore	stair
stare	stake	steak
sundae	Sunday	tee
tea	throne	thrown

tide	tied	tow
toe	wail	whale
waste	waist	week
weak	wine	whine
yoke	yolk	

Chapter 15. Present Perfect Speed — Directions

OBJECTIVE:

To practice present perfect irregular verbs.

HOW TO PREPARE FOR THIS LESSON:

Photocopy and cut out the **Present Perfect Speed** Game Cards.

NOW BEGIN:

Divide the class into two teams. Two players from one team sit at the front of the class.

Place the stack of game cards, face down, in front of Player A. Time each round for 45 seconds. When the round begins, Player A picks a game card and reads the top sentence. Player B must repeat the sentence but replace the future tense of the verb with the present perfect tense.

For example:

Player A: "**I will teach** this class."
Player B: "**I have taught** this class."

If Player B does this correctly, Player A puts the game card to one side of the table and their team earns a point. If not, the card goes to the other side of the table. At the end of the round, the two players return to their seats and two new players from the opposing team go to the front to start a new round. The team with the most points wins.

Page 157

A Bright Idea!

For an added twist, you may want to give Team B, the team not playing, a chance to steal some points from the pile of incorrectly answered game chips.

After the round is over, Team B can, without the pressure of being timed, try to correctly answer these game chips.

This will motivate Team A to try especially hard to give the correct answers and not let any points go to Team B.

This will also motivate Team B to pay closer attention even if it's not their turn to play.

Cheater Alert!

Most bilingual dictionaries contain an exhaustive list of conjugated verbs. These are not to be used during this lesson.

Chapter 15. Present Perfect Speed Game Cards #1

They **will lose** the game.	I **will pay** the bill.	The kids **will grow** fast.
They **have lost** the game.	I **have paid** the bill.	The kids **have grown** fast.
He **will swing** the bat.	I **will run** 5 miles.	He **will quit** his job.
He **has swung** the bat.	I **have run** 5 miles.	He **has quit** his job.
He **will stand** in line.	He **will rewrite** the paper.	The ship **will sink**.
He **has stood** in line.	He **has rewritten** the paper.	The ship **has sunk**.
She **will steal** the money.	We **will rebuild** the house.	They **will sew** the costumes.
She **has stolen** the money.	We **have rebuilt** the house.	They **have sewn** the costumes.
The food **will spoil**.	We **will set** the table.	She **will take** a walk.
The food **has spoiled**.	We **have set** the table.	She **has taken** a walk.
The bee **will sting** me.	I **will withdraw** the money.	I **will run** for president.
The bee **has stung** me.	I **have withdrawn** the money.	I **have run** for president.

Chapter 15. **Present Perfect Speed** Game Cards #2

You **will read** the report.	You **will throw** a party.	You **will give** the gift.
You **have read** the report.	You **have thrown** a party.	You **have given** the gift.
You **will say** it in Spanish.	You **will bring** the wine.	You **will make** a plan.
You **have said** it in Spanish.	You **have brought** the wine.	You **have made** a plan.
You **will meet** her parents.	You **will lead** the group.	You **will drive** a car.
You **have met** her parents.	You **have led** the group.	You **have driven** a car.
You **will go** to the store.	You **will see** the play.	You **will win** the game.
You **have gone** to the store.	You **have seen** the play.	You **have won** the game.
I **will eat** the apples.	I **will have** a cup of tea.	I **will sleep** in the tent.
I **have eaten** the apples.	I **have had** a cup of tea.	I **have slept** in the tent.
We **will quit** smoking.	We **will sit** on the bench.	We **will send** the letter.
We **have quit** smoking.	We **have sat** on the bench.	We **have sent** the letter.

Chapter 15.   **Present Perfect Speed**   Game Cards #3

I **will swim** at the beach.	I **will live** in Paris.	I **will throw** the ball.
I **have swum** at the beach.	I **have lived** in Paris.	I **have thrown** the ball.
I **will speak** Italian.	I **will bring** donuts.	I **will sing** at the club.
I **have spoken** Italian.	I **have brought** donuts.	I **have sung** at the club.
I **will buy** new shoes.	I **will take** the train.	I **will fly** to London.
I **have bought** new shoes.	I **have taken** the train.	I **have flown** to London.
She **will leave** this town.	She **will mow** the grass.	She **will lend** us her car.
She **has left** this town.	She **has mowed** the grass.	She **has lent** us her car.
The phone **will ring**.	She **will pay** the rent.	She **will run** in the race.
The phone **has rung**.	She **has paid** the rent.	She **has run** in the race.
We **will shut** the doors.	We **will spend** the money.	We **will set** the table.
We **have shut** the doors.	We **have spent** the money.	We **have set** the table.

Chapter 15. **Present Perfect Speed** Game Cards #4  Page 161

The sun **will rise**.	She **will sell** her house.	She **will take** a class.
The sun **has risen**.	She **has sold** her house.	She **has taken** a class.
She **will wear** the dress.	She **will write** a book.	She **will think** about it.
She **has worn** the dress.	She **has written** a book.	She **has thought** about it.
He **will tell** us the news.	He **will swing** at the ball.	He **will teach** us French.
He **has told** us the news.	He **has swung** at the ball.	He **has taught** us French.
He **will sweep** the floor.	He **will stand** at the door.	He **will bet** on that horse.
He **has swept** the floor.	He **has stood** at the door.	He **has bet** on that horse.
It **will be** a busy day.	He **will build** a new house.	He **will choose** that one.
It **has been** a busy day.	He **has built** a new house.	He **has chosen** that one.
We **will show** them how.	We **will slide** down the hill.	We **will beat** that team.
We **have shown** them how.	We **have slid** down the hill.	We **have beaten** that team.

Chapter 15. Present Perfect Speed Game Cards #5

He **will draw** a picture.	He **will dig** a hole.	He **will feel** better.
He **has drawn** a picture.	He **has dug** a hole.	He **has felt** better.
They **will keep** the secret.	They **will break** the toy.	They **will breed** dogs.
They **have kept** the secret.	They **have broken** the toy.	They **have bred** dogs.
They **will catch** the thief.	They **will come** in.	They **will do** the work.
They **have caught** the thief.	They **have come** in.	They **have done** the work.
They **will drink** some tea.	They **will feed** the dogs.	They **will find** a clue.
They **have drunk** some tea.	They **have fed** the dogs.	They **have found** a clue.
They **will hear** a speech.	They **will know** the truth.	They **will light** the candles.
They **have heard** a speech.	They **have known** the truth.	They **have lit** the candles.
We **will slay** the dragons.	We **will hang** the pictures.	We **will swear** on The Bible.
We **have slain** the dragons.	We **have hung** the pictures.	We **have sworn** on The Bible.

Chapter 16. **Grocery Shopping**   Directions

Objective:

To get students more comfortable with the language of shopping, using U.S. currency, expanding their food-related vocabulary, and negotiation.

How to prepare for this lesson:

Photocopy enough **Grocery Shopping** Study Sheets for each student and yourself. Go over this sheet as a class.

Divide the class in half—Customers and Shopkeepers.

Each Shopkeeper gets one pre-cut sheet of one dollar bills and accompanying coins and one sheet of five dollar bills and accompanying coins (page 237). Each Shopkeeper should start the game with the same amount of money. Make two photocopies each of the **Grocery Shopping** Food Cards, cut them up, shuffle, and deal them out to the Shopkeepers. Provide scratch paper so the Shopkeepers can display prices for their food items if they want.

Hand out a **Grocery Shopping** Grocery List card and a twenty dollar bill (page 240) to every Customer. Explain that the Grocery List card shows the items they need to buy to win the game. The twenty dollar bill is all they'll have to purchase what's on their list.

Page 163

Prior to this Lesson:

Depending on the level of your students, it might be best to complete:

○ 1-2-3- Write!

○ ZINGO!

○ Exact Change

prior to doing this lesson.

Note:

This lesson is intended for larger classes—6 students or more.

If you have an odd number of students, have the majority be Customers.

If you have a very large class, Make 2 copies of the Grocery Lists and 4 copies of the Food Cards. You could also have students shop in pairs and/or have Shopkeepers work in pairs.

Chapter 16. **Grocery Shopping** Directions

Page 164

Business Relevance

The business relevance of this lesson is learning negotiation and compromise (or cut-throat business tactics such as price gouging depending on the individual and circumstances).

Make it clear to the class that this is not a speed game. This is a game of negotiation.

Caution !

Depending on the nationality of your students, you may want to make it clear that bartering and haggling over prices is not, in fact, a common practice in most Western countries.

Now begin:

Of the Customers, the person who can complete their grocery list while spending the least amount of money wins.

Of the Shopkeepers, the one to have the most cash (not including the value of unsold food) at the end of the game wins.

The Shopkeepers can set and change their prices as they like. The Customers can try to haggle prices down. Both the Customers and Shopkeepers can barter—either between Customer and Shopkeeper, between Customers, or between Shopkeepers.

Try to have the Shopkeepers set up shop as far away from each other as possible. Each Shopkeeper should have some surface, like a desk, on which to display their wares (food cards) and prices.

For an interactive, on-line activity, try:

○ ProfessorMelonhead.com/Spelling_FruitVeg.html

Grocery Shopping   Study Sheet

Questions	Statements	Negative Statements
Do you have any sugar?	I need some sugar.	I don't need any sugar.
Do you have any onions?	I need two onions.	I don't need any onions.
Do you need any corn?	I have an ear of corn.	I don't have any corn.
Do you need any garlic?	I have a bulb of garlic.	I don't have any garlic.

Shopping Dialogue

Mr. Chen: Do you need any potatoes?

Ms. Garcia: No, thank you. I don't need any potatoes but I do need some sugar. Do you have any sugar?

Mr. Chen: Yes, I do. Here you go. Do you need any corn? I'm having a sale—two ears of corn for a dollar.

Ms. Garcia: Okay. I'll have two ears of corn.

Mr. Chen: Would you like anything else?

Ms. Garcia: No, thank you.

Mr. Chen: Your total is $3.45.

Ms. Garcia: Here's five dollars.

Mr. Chen: Your change is $1.55.

Ms. Garcia: Thank you.

Mr. Chen: You're welcome and please come again.

Chapter 16. **Grocery Shopping** Grocery Lists #1

Grocery List #1

- [ ] peas
- [ ] potatoes
- [ ] beans
- [ ] cherries
- [ ] a cantaloupe
- [ ] leeks
- [ ] tomatoes
- [ ] cauliflower
- [ ] corn
- [ ] a pear

Grocery List #2

- [ ] bananas
- [ ] cherries
- [ ] an artichoke
- [ ] asparagus
- [ ] cabbage
- [ ] a squash
- [ ] potatoes
- [ ] an apple
- [ ] a sweet potato
- [ ] radishes

Grocery List #3

- [ ] grapes
- [ ] a pumpkin
- [ ] a sweet potato
- [ ] asparagus
- [ ] strawberries
- [ ] a lemon
- [ ] mushrooms
- [ ] an apple
- [ ] celery
- [ ] an orange

Grocery List #4

- [ ] celery
- [ ] rice
- [ ] leeks
- [ ] a lemon
- [ ] a watermelon
- [ ] garlic
- [ ] beans
- [ ] plums
- [ ] an eggplant
- [ ] carrots

Chapter 16. **Grocery Shopping** Grocery Lists #2

Grocery List #5

- ☐ plums
- ☐ a zucchini
- ☐ rice
- ☐ onions
- ☐ a cucumber
- ☐ grapes
- ☐ tomatoes
- ☐ an orange
- ☐ a pear
- ☐ bananas

Grocery List #6

- ☐ onions
- ☐ carrots
- ☐ an artichoke
- ☐ bananas
- ☐ peppers
- ☐ a squash
- ☐ potatoes
- ☐ an apple
- ☐ cauliflower
- ☐ radishes

Grocery List #7

- ☐ mushrooms
- ☐ a cucumber
- ☐ broccoli
- ☐ rice
- ☐ strawberries
- ☐ garlic
- ☐ peppers
- ☐ peas
- ☐ an eggplant
- ☐ radishes

Grocery List #8

- ☐ a pumpkin
- ☐ broccoli
- ☐ a zucchini
- ☐ garlic
- ☐ a watermelon
- ☐ a cantaloupe
- ☐ potatoes
- ☐ corn
- ☐ an eggplant
- ☐ asparagus

 Chapter 16. **Grocery Shopping** Food Cards #1

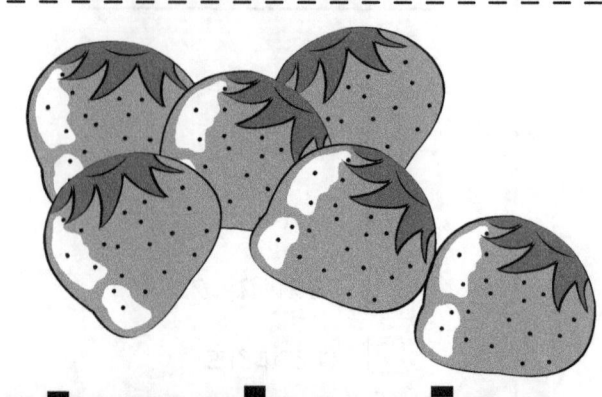
strawberries

grapes

bananas

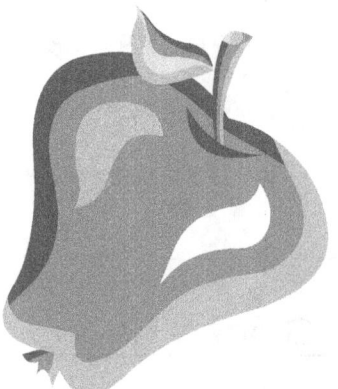
apple

pear

orange

Chapter 16. **Grocery Shopping** Food Cards #2

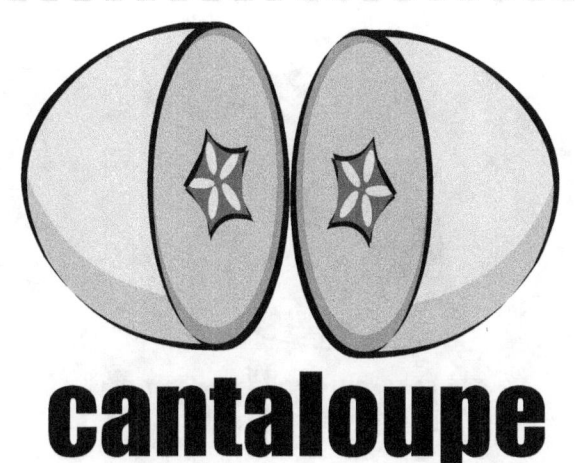
cantaloupe

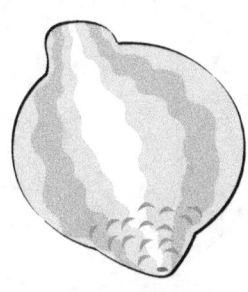
lemon

plums

cherries

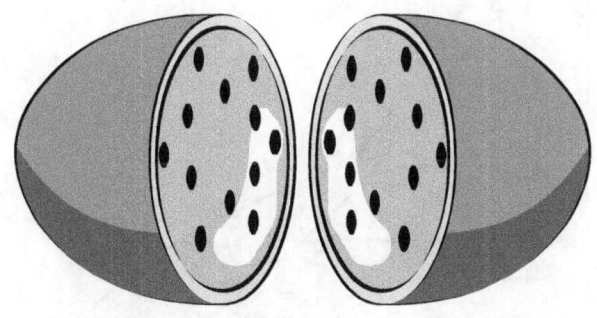
watermelon

beans

Chapter 16. **Grocery Shopping**   Food Cards #3

cabbage

eggplant

pumpkin

cucumber

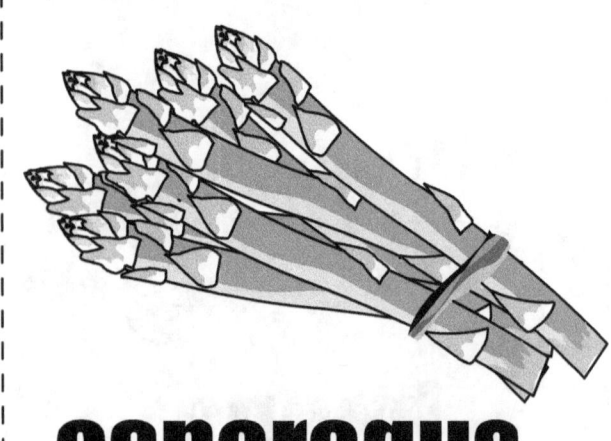
asparagus

corn

Chapter 16. **Grocery Shopping**   Food Cards #4   Page 171

peas

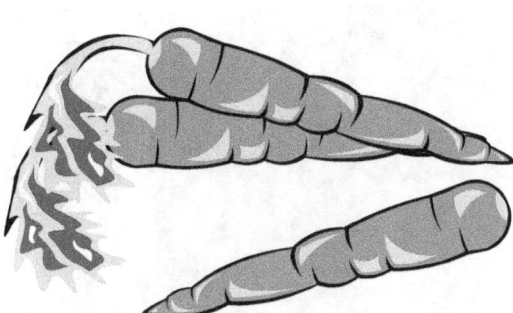
carrots

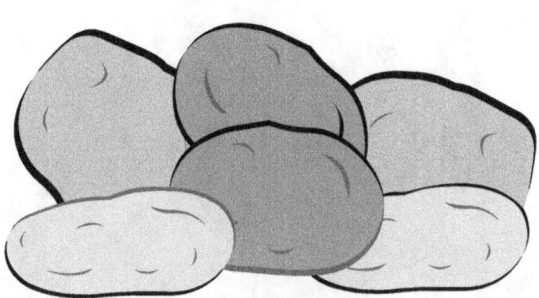
potatoes

peppers

onions

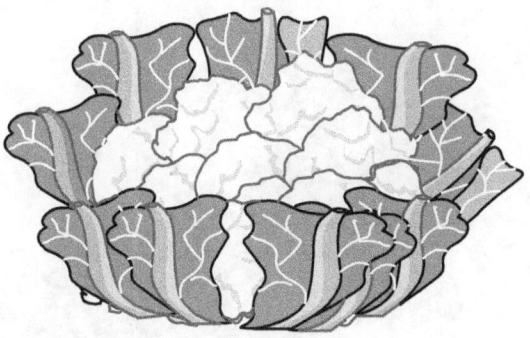
cauliflower

Chapter 16.   **Grocery Shopping**   Food Cards #5

tomatoes

garlic

radishes

artichoke

celery

rice

Chapter 16. **Grocery Shopping** Food Cards #6

broccoli

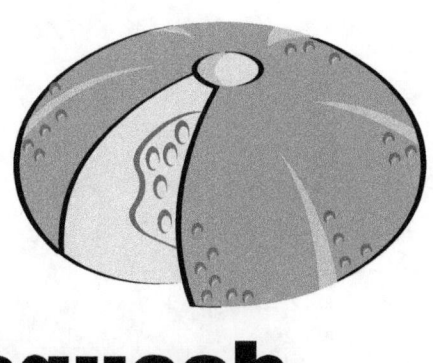
squash

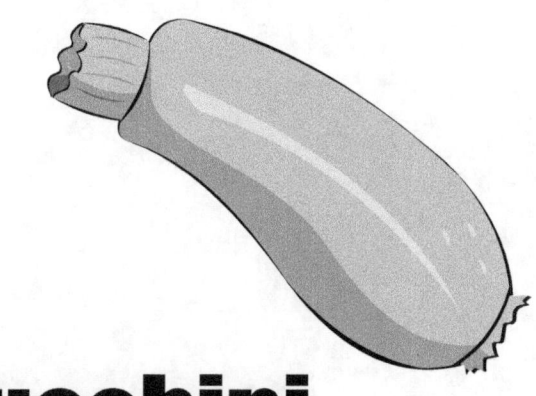
zucchini

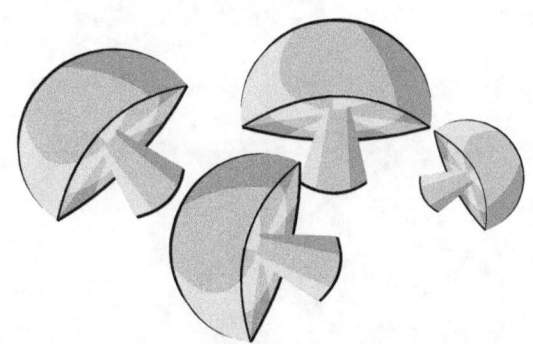
mushrooms

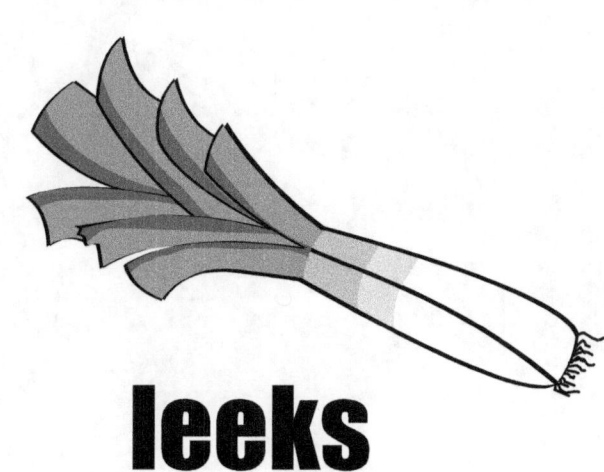
leeks

sweet potato

Chapter 17. What's Cooking?   Directions

OBJECTIVE:

To teach students how to explain a process clearly so that others can understand it, while bolstering listening comprehension skills and learning common cooking-related verbs.

HOW TO PREPARE FOR THIS LESSON:

Photocopy enough **What's Cooking?** Study Sheets for each student and yourself. This is mostly dictionary work, so my preference would be to hand it out for homework the previous week rather than devote too much class time to it.

List commonly prepared meals that most of the class is likely to be familiar with. A Blank Game Chips sheet is included (page 248) for you to list additional dishes not found in this book.

If you are teaching in a foreign country, this gives you the perfect excuse to familiarize yourself with the national and/or regional cuisine. If you are teaching in your home country, this is a good opportunity to anoint yourself "(Your Nationality Here)_____ Cuisine Ambassador."

NOW BEGIN:

Divide your class into groups of 3-5. Place each set of game cards, face down, before each group. One person from each group randomly chooses a game

---

Page 175

Prior to this Lesson:

Depending on the level of your students, it might be best to complete:

- Grocery Shopping

prior to doing this lesson, for basic food vocabulary.

Business Relevance

This lesson is an enjoyable and relaxing warm-up to lessons in which students explain other processes to their classmates, for example, describing their job in detail or a particular project they have been assigned to.

Chapter 17. What's Cooking?   Directions

Page 176

A Bright Idea !

If you would like to use this format but feel that explaining a process such as cooking is too ambitious for your students, try something easier like describing household items or things found in an office.

Have a clearly defined theme to give the lesson some structure and make it easier for the class to focus on specific vocabulary.

A **Blank Game Chips** sheet is located in the Appendix (page 248).

A Bright Idea !

Photocopy or print a couple of recipes in English for the class to use as a point of reference.

card and tries to describe how the dish written on the card is prepared. The other members of the group try to be the first to guess what that dish is, based on his/her description. The first one to guess coreectly is the next person to choose a new card and describe a new dish.

What's Cooking?   Study Sheet

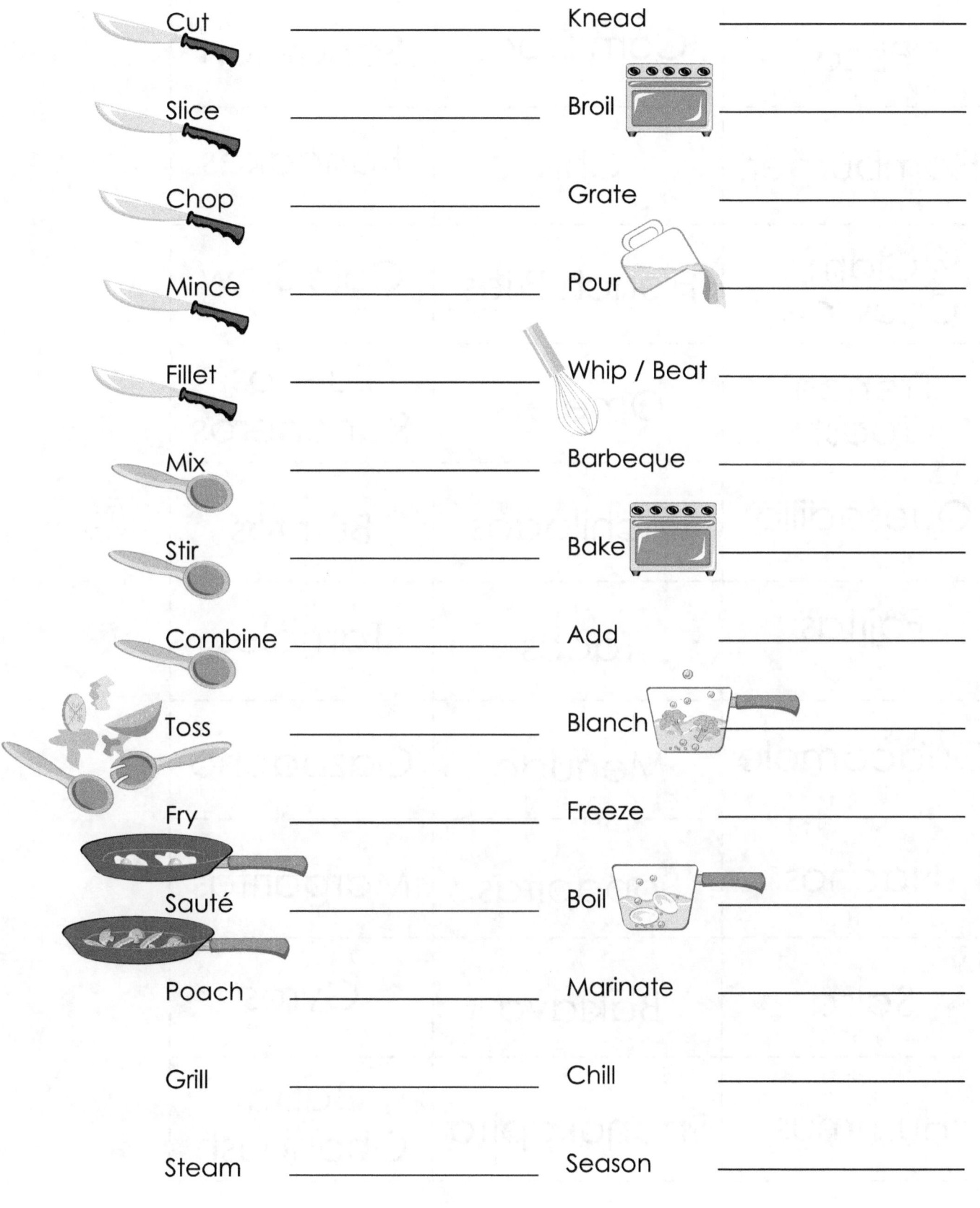

Cut	_____	Knead	_____
Slice	_____	Broil	_____
Chop	_____	Grate	_____
Mince	_____	Pour	_____
Fillet	_____	Whip / Beat	_____
Mix	_____	Barbeque	_____
Stir	_____	Bake	_____
Combine	_____	Add	_____
Toss	_____	Blanch	_____
Fry	_____	Freeze	_____
Sauté	_____	Boil	_____
Poach	_____	Marinate	_____
Grill	_____	Chill	_____
Steam	_____	Season	_____

FUN, QUICK & EASY   Game-Based Activities for Teachers of Adult ESL   Page 177

Pizza	Corn Dogs	Sandwich
Hamburger	Chili	Pancakes
Clam Chowder	French Fries	Cole Slaw
French Toast	Omelets	Juevos Rancheros
Quesadilla	Enchiladas	Burritos
Fajitas	Tacos	Tamales
Guacamole	Menudo	Gazpacho
Nachos	Sopapitas	Margaritas
Salsa	Baklava	Gyros
Hummus	Spanokopita	Baba Ghanoush

Calzones	Cannolis	Frittata
Lasagna	Spaghetti	Tiramisu
Fried Rice	Egg Rolls	Ramen
Crepes	Croissant	Custard
Curry	Naan	Samosas
Sauerkraut	Pretzels	Pad Thai
Sushi	Sukiyaki	Yakisoba
Chanko	Shabu Shabu	Kurikinton
Takoyaki	Tempura	Oden
Mochi	Okonomiyaki	Taiyaki

Chapter 17. **What's Cooking?** Game Sheet #3

Falafel	Trifle	Roly-poly
Crumpets	Yorkshire Pudding	Pastie
Spotted Dick	Bubble & Squeak	Toad-in-the-Hole
Hasty Pudding	Pavlova	Shephard's Pie
Anzac Biscuits	Lamingtons	Dumplings
Knish	Fatayer	Latkes
Rugelach	Hush Puppies	Gumbo
Succotash	Haggis	Stovies
Bridie	Cullen Skink	Mince Pie
Champ	Colcannon	Simnel Cake

Chapter 18. Talking Trivia — Directions

Business Relevance

This is good practice to encourage students to listen carefully to someone asking them a question in English and then give an accurate response.

During business dealings the ability to pay close attention to what another person is saying and to accurately answer questions is vital.

OBJECTIVE:

To improve reading and listening comprehension skills and expand vocabulary.

HOW TO PREPARE FOR THIS LESSON:

Compile a list of trivia questions and their corresponding answers. Sample trivia questions are included in this chapter.

Print out your trivia sheets and cut them into their individual questions and corresponding answers.

NOW BEGIN:

Break the class into groups of at least three. Give each group their trivia questions, face down.

Student A picks a question from the pile and reads it to Student B. If Student B answers the question correctly, Student B keeps the paper and thus earns a point. If not, the point is dead and moved off to the side of the table. Student B picks a question and reads it to Student C and so on. The student with the most pieces of paper at the end of the game wins.

Your role is to explain the meaning of the trivia questions if needed.

Business Relevance

If all of your students are from the same company, try to include some company-related trivia questions and answers. This will help make the lesson more relevant to their professional life. For example, "When was your company founded?", "Where are your headquarters located?"

(...and it's loads of fun for the corporate underlings to watch their managers squirm if they can't answer basic questions about the company.)

Chapter 18. **Talking Trivia** Game Sheet #1 World Geography

Question:
What is the only country that borders both Venezuela & Paraguay?

Answer:
Brazil.

Question:
What is the only country that borders both Vietnam & Nepal?

Answer:
China.

Question:
What is the only country that borders both Belize & El Salvador?

Answer:
Guatemala.

Question:
What is the only country that borders both Indonesia & Thailand?

Answer:
Malaysia.

Question:
What is the only country that borders both France & Spain?

Answer:
Andorra.

Question:
What is the only country that borders both North Korea & Finland?

Answer:
Russia.

Question:
What is the only country that borders both Lesotho & Swaziland?

Answer:
South Africa.

Question:
What is the only country that borders both Iraq & Greece?

Answer:
Turkey.

Question:
What is the only country that borders both Chile & Peru?

Answer:
Bolivia.

Question:
What is the only country that borders both the Dem. Rep. of Congo & Egypt?

Answer:
Sudan.

Chapter 18. **Talking Trivia**   Game Sheet #2   U.S. Geography

Question:
Which 2 states of the United States of America begin with the word "North"?

Answer:
North Carolina and North Dakota.

Question:
Which 2 states of the United States of America begin with the word "South"?

Answer:
South Carolina and South Dakota.

Question:
Which state of the United States of America begins with the word "West"?

Answer:
West Virginia.

Question:
Which 4 states of the United States of America begin with the word "New"?

Answer:
New Hampshire, New Jersey, New Mexico, and New York.

Question:
Which 2 states of the United States of America are not part of the continental United States?

Answer:
Hawaii and Alaska.

Question:
What is the capital of the United States of America?

Answer:
Washington D.C.

Question:
How many states are in the United States of America?

Answer:
Fifty.

Question:
Which state of the Unites States of America is the smallest?

Answer:
Rhode Island.

Question:
Which state of the Unites States of America is the largest?

Answer:
Alaska.

Question:
Which 2 countries border the United States of America?

Answer:
Canada to the north and Mexico to the south.

Chapter 18. **Talking Trivia** Game Sheet #3 U.S. Geography

Question:
How do you spell Wyoming?

Answer:
W-Y-O-M-I-N-G.

Question:
How do you spell Missouri?

Answer:
M-I-S-S-O-U-R-I.

Question:
How do you spell Arkansas?

Answer:
A-R-K-A-N-S-A-S.

Question:
How do you spell California?

Answer:
C-A-L-I-F-O-R-N-I-A.

Question:
How do you spell Louisiana?

Answer:
L-O-U-I-S-I-A-N-A.

Question:
How do you spell Massachusetts?

Answer:
M-A-S-S-A-C-H-U-S-E-T-T-S.

Question:
How do you spell Mississippi?

Answer:
M-I-S-S-I-S-S-I-P-P-I.

Question:
How do you spell Tennessee?

Answer:
T-E-N-N-E-S-S-E-E.

Question:
How do you spell Pennsylvania?

Answer:
P-E-N-N-S-Y-L-V-A-N-I-A.

Question:
How do you spell Connecticut?

Answer:
C-O-N-N-E-C-T-I-C-U-T.

Chapter 18.   **Talking Trivia**   Game Sheet #4   U.S. Geography

Question: Is Texas a northern state or a southern state?	**Question:** Is California on the east coast or the west coast of the United States?
Answer: A southern state.	**Answer:** West coast.
Question: Is Montana a northern state or a southern state?	**Question:** Is New York on the east coast or the west coast of the United States?
Answer: A northern state.	**Answer:** East coast.
Question: Is Louisiana a northern state or a southern state?	**Question:** Is Oregon on the east coast or the west coast of the United States?
Answer: A southern state.	**Answer:** West coast.
Question: Is Minnesota a northern state or a southern state?	**Question:** Is Pennsylvania on the east coast or the west coast of the United States?
Answer: A northern state.	**Answer:** East coast.
Question: Is Florida a northern state or a southern state?	**Question:** Is Connecticut on the east coast or the west coast of the United States?
Answer: A southern state.	**Answer:** East coast.

Chapter 18. **Talking Trivia** Game Sheet #5 Americana

Question: The Statue of Liberty was a gift to the United States from what country?	**Question:** Who were the first three presidents of the United States of America?
Answer: France.	**Answer:** 1. George Washington, 2. John Adams, 3. Thomas Jefferson.
Question: What is the motto of the United States of America?	**Question:** How many years is one presidential term?
Answer: "In God We Trust."	**Answer:** Four years.
Question: How many stripes are on the flag of the United States of America?	**Question:** Which state was the last state to become part of the United States of America?
Answer: Thirteen—representing the original 13 colonies.	**Answer:** Hawaii.
Question: How many stars are on the flag of the United States of America?	**Question:** Las Vegas is a city in which state?
Answer: Fifty—representing the 50 states.	**Answer:** Nevada.
Question: What is the national bird of the United States of America?	**Question:** Los Angeles is a city in which state?
Answer: The bald eagle.	**Answer:** California.

Chapter 18. **Talking Trivia** Game Sheet #6 International Currency

Question: What is the currency of the United States of America?	**Question:** What is the currency of Argentina?
Answer: The U.S. dollar.	**Answer:** The peso.
Question: What is the currency of India?	**Question:** What is the currency of Iraq?
Answer: The rupee.	**Answer:** The dinar.
Question: What is the currency of Japan?	**Question:** What is the currency of Iran?
Answer: The yen.	**Answer:** The rial.
Question: What is the currency of Mexico?	**Question:** What is the currency of South Africa?
Answer: The peso.	**Answer:** The rand.
Question: What is the currency of France?	**Question:** What is the currency of Jamaica?
Answer: The euro.	**Answer:** The dollar.

Chapter 18. **Talking Trivia** Game Sheet #7 International Currency

Question: What is the currency of China?	**Question:** What is the currency of Brazil?
Answer: The yuan.	**Answer:** The real.
Question: What is the currency of South Korea?	**Question:** What is the currency of Afghanistan?
Answer: The won.	**Answer:** The afghani.
Question: What is the currency of Vietnam?	**Question:** What is the currency of Cuba?
Answer: The dong.	**Answer:** The peso.
Question: What is the currency of Israel?	**Question:** What is the currency of Ethiopia?
Answer: The (new) shekel.	**Answer:** The birr.
Question: What is the currency of Egypt?	**Question:** What is the currency of Uganda?
Answer: The pound.	**Answer:** The shilling.

Chapter 18. **Talking Trivia** Game Sheet #8 Miscellaneous

Question: Planet Earth is between which two planets?	**Question:** Which two planets in our solar system have no moons?
Answer: Venus and Mars.	**Answer:** Venus and Mercury.
Question: Name the author of the Harry Potter books.	**Question:** What is the highest mountain in the world?
Answer: J.K. Rowling.	**Answer:** Mount Everest.
Question: Name all 4 members of The Beatles.	**Question:** In the United States, Thanksgiving is celebrated on what day?
Answer: John Lennon, Paul McCartney, Ringo Starr, and George Harrison.	**Answer:** The 4th Thursday in November.
Question: Who directed the famous horror films *Vertigo*, *Psycho*, and *The Birds*?	**Question:** Who was the first astronaut on the moon?
Answer: Alfred Hitchcock.	**Answer:** Neil Armstrong.
Question: The western holiday, Halloween, is celebrated on what day?	**Question:** What is the best hand in a game of Poker?
Answer: October 31st.	**Answer:** A Royal Flush—Ace, King, Queen, Jack, Ten, and Nine, all of the same suit.

Chapter 18. **Talking Trivia**   Game Sheet #9   Nations' Capitals

Question:
What is the capital of Japan?

Answer:
Tokyo.

Question:
What is the capital of Brazil?

Answer:
Brasilia.

Question:
What is the capital of Afghanistan?

Answer:
Kabul.

Question:
What is the capital of China?

Answer:
Beijing.

Question:
What is the capital of Iran?

Answer:
Tehran.

Question:
What is the capital of Thailand?

Answer:
Bangkok.

Question:
What is the capital of Iraq?

Answer:
Baghdad.

Question:
What is the capital of Turkey?

Answer:
Ankara.

Question:
What is the capital of Germany?

Answer:
Berlin.

Question:
What is the capital of Scotland?

Answer:
Edinburgh.

Chapter 18. **Talking Trivia**   Game Sheet #10   Nations' Capitals

Question: What is the capital of Iceland?	**Question:** What is the capital of Cuba?
Answer: Reykjavik.	**Answer:** Havana.
Question: What is the capital of Israel?	**Question:** What is the capital of Egypt?
Answer: Jerusalem.	**Answer:** Cairo.
Question: What is the capital of Ireland?	**Question:** What is the capital of Ethiopia?
Answer: Dublin.	**Answer:** Addis Ababa.
Question: What is the capital of India?	**Question:** What is the capital of Pakistan?
Answer: New Delhi.	**Answer:** Islamabad.
Question: What is the capital of Australia?	**Question:** What is the capital of Canada?
Answer: Canberra.	**Answer:** Ottawa.

Chapter 18. **Talking Trivia** Game Sheet #11 Celebrity Real Names

---

Question:
Thomas Mapotheer IV is better known as...

Answer:
Tom Cruise.

Question:
Allen Konigsberg is better known as...

Answer:
Woody Allen.

Question:
David Robert Jones is better known as...

Answer:
David Bowie.

Question:
Archibald Leach is better known as...

Answer:
Cary Grant.

Question:
Calvin Broadus is better known as...

Answer:
Snoop Doggy Dog.

Question:
Chan Kwong-Sung is better known as...

Answer:
Jackie Chan.

Question:
Paul Hewson is better known as...

Answer:
Bono (lead singer of the band U2).

Question:
Margaret Hyra is better known as...

Answer:
Meg Ryan.

Question:
Robert Zimmerman is better known as...

Answer:
Bob Dylan.

Question:
Lee Yuen Kam is better known as...

Answer:
Bruce Lee.

Chapter 19. Whisper Directions

OBJECTIVE:

For large high school or vocational college classes when pre-test review is required.

HOW TO PREPARE FOR THIS LESSON:

Compile a list of sentences—ideally, sentences that are relevant examples of grammar they should know for a test. How many sentences you'll need depends on the length of the class but plan on having about 10-12 sentences ready per class hour.

Preferably, you'll want groups of 4-6 students. Therefore, if you have a class of 25 kids with five students per group, you'll need five copies of your sentences. Cut them into their individual sentences.

Make sure you have enough chalk or whiteboard pens for each group. If you don't think you'll have enough board space for each student, then use a table with blank sheets of paper and pencils with erasures.

NOW BEGIN:

Have the students arrange their chairs in straight rows, from the head of the class to the back of the class. Then call the first person from each row to the

---

Page 193

Save A Tree

The question strips you create for this lesson will very likely be tossed in the rubbish can at the end of this lesson. Therefore, consider using recycled office paper.

As long as the paper isn't too crumpled (i.e. can be sent through a printer or copy machine) and has one clean side, you can print your questions on the other side.

The students will hardly notice or care that you're using recycled paper.

Chapter 19. **Whisper** Directions

Page 194

Cheater Alert!

Make sure the students clear their desks as much as possible. I've had students try to write the sentences on loose scratch paper and just hand the written sentence to the next person. In large classrooms this is not always easy to catch.

Caution!

Depending on the country you're teaching in or the cultural background of your students, whispering into the ear of someone of the opposite sex may be a big no-no.

If in doubt, ask someone qualified to give a well-informed opinion on this matter.

head of the class and hand them each the first sentence. It's important that they all get the same sentence. Tell them to memorize the sentence, collect the papers back from them, and they can return to their seats, facing forward.

When you say "Go!", they must turn around and whisper the sentence they have just read to the person behind them, who must then whisper the same sentence to the person behind them. The last person in the row must then go to the front of the class and write the sentence perfectly on the board. The first team to write the sentence perfectly earns a point.

When the first round is complete, have the students rotate so that the last person in the row is now the first and must go to the front of the class to read the next sentence. The students who were in the first seats should now be in the second seats, the students in the second seats should now be in the third seats, and so on.

While the students are at the board, it would be best to stay out of their way unless they yell that they've finished. If there are errors in the sentence, simply underline those errors and wordlessly move away. You've presumably already taught the grammar. This is review; it's now on their shoulders to figure it out.

You Must Be Joking

Chapter 20. You Must Be Joking — Directions

OBJECTIVE:

To be able to read and get the gist of a joke and then clearly and effectively relate that information to the rest of the class.

A joke telling lesson helps to develop reading and listening comprehension skills and gives the class a peek into Western culture through humor.

HOW TO PREPARE FOR THIS LESSON:

Decide on a theme for your jokes (work, marriage, politics, etc.) and collect about four or five pages of jokes of various lengths and difficulty. A bit of internet surfing will likely provide you with more jokes than you can handle. Sample jokes are included at the end of this chapter.

Organize your jokes onto one document, leaving enough space between jokes for cutting. Print your joke pages and cut them into individual jokes.

Begin your lesson by asking your students if anyone can tell you a joke in English. Don't be surprised if no one is able to offer a joke at this time. Have a warm-up joke memorized to tell to the class. See if they get the joke. If not, explain it to them.

Explain that jokes are often in threes and therefore can be easier to memorize. For example, "Three guys

Business Relevance

A joke-telling lesson is a fun and relaxing way to get students used to public speaking and/or a business meeting format.

It requires each student to process information (the joke) fairly quickly and then effectively and accurately relay that information to a group of people.

The audience must pay close attention to the speaker and ask clarifying questions if they don't get the joke.

Chapter 20. You Must Be Joking - Directions

Page 198

Caution !

Know Your Audience! Use your common sense and good taste when selecting jokes for your class. Jokes that demean people (e.g., jokes that are sexist, racist, homophobic, etc.) should be avoided. Jokes that use profanity or are vulgar or racy (e.g., dirty jokes) should also be avoided. Jokes poking fun at popular religious leaders could get you into serious trouble as well.

A joke-telling lesson is best after you have spent some time with your students and have a good feel for their sensibilities.

walk into a bar. The first guy says 'blah,' the second guy says 'blah,' and the third guy says 'blah.'" Explain what a punch line is.

Spend some time going over the theme of your jokes. For example, for jokes on political humor, ask your students to explain the difference between liberals and conservatives. Ask them what the two main political parties of the United States are and what they represent. Ask each student if they are more liberal or conservative in their political views and why.

Hand out the first round of jokes. Make these the shortest jokes in the pile. Have the students read their joke to themselves, then quietly go around to each student to make sure they understand why it's funny. When you are sure that each student understands his/her joke, have each student tell his/her joke to the class. Have other students explain why each joke is funny to be sure each joke is understood.

They will probably want to read their jokes word-for-word from the paper. This is fine for the first round but as the class progresses, wean them from using the paper as a crutch. By the last few rounds they should be able to relate their jokes without looking at their paper at all.

Chapter 20. **You Must Be Joking** Work #1

Job Application

Two young engineers applied for a single position at a computer company. They both had the same qualifications. In order to determine which individual to hire, the applicants were asked to take a test by the department manager. Upon completion of the test, both men had each missed only one of the questions.

The manager went to the first applicant and said, "Thank you for your interest, but we've decided to give the job to the other applicant."

"And why would you be doing that? We both got nine questions correct," asked the rejected applicant.

"We have based our decision not on the correct answers, but on the question you missed," said the department manager.

"And just how would one incorrect answer be better than the other?" the rejected applicant inquired.

"Simple," said the department manager, "Your fellow applicant put down on question #5, 'I don't know.' You put down, 'Neither do I.'"

Earring

A man is at work one day when he notices that his co-worker is wearing an earring. This man knows his co-worker to be a somewhat conservative fellow, so naturally he's curious about the sudden change in fashion sense. The man walks up to his co-worker and says, "I didn't know you were into earrings."

"Don't make such a big deal, it's only an earring," he replies sheepishly.

"Well, I'm curious," begged the man, "how long have you been wearing an earring?"

"Er, ever since my wife found it in our bed."

A Smart Saleswoman!

A neatly dressed saleswoman stopped a man in the street and asked, "Sir, would you like to buy a bottle of this mouthwash for $200?" Aghast, the man said, "Are you NUTS? That's robbery!"

The saleswoman seemed hurt and then tried again. "Sir, since you are a bit irate, I'll sell it to you for 1/2 price at $100." Again, the man replied bluntly, "You must be crazy, lady, now go away!"

The saleswoman then reaches into her briefcase and pulls out two brownies and begins munching away on one of them. She tells the irate guy, "Sir, please share one of my brownies since I have annoyed you so much."

Unwrapping the brownie, the guy takes a bite. Suddenly, the guys spits it out. "HEY," he snarls, "this brownie tastes like crap!!!"

"It is," replied the saleswoman. "Wanna buy some mouthwash?"

May I Take Your Order?

A customer walks into a restaurant and notices a large sign on the wall: $500 IF WE FAIL TO FILL YOUR ORDER!

When his waitress arrives, he orders elephant dung on rye. She calmly writes down his order and walks into the kitchen where all hell breaks loose!

The restaurant owner comes storming out of the kitchen. He runs up to the customer's table, slaps five $100 bills down on it and says, "You got me that time, buddy, but I want you to know that's the first time in ten years we've been out of rye bread!"

Chapter 20. **You Must Be Joking** Work #3

The Taxi Ride

A cabbie picks up a tourist in New York on a dark night. The passenger taps the driver on the shoulder to ask him something.

The driver screams, loses control of the car, nearly hits a bus, drives up on the sidewalk, and stops, inches from a shop window.

For a second, everything goes quiet in the cab. Then the driver says, "Look, ma'am, don't EVER do that again. You scared the daylights out of me!"

The passenger apologizes and says she didn't realize that a little tap could scare him so much. The driver, after gathering himself together replies, "Sorry, it's not really your fault. Today is my first day as a cab driver—I've been driving hearses for the last 25 years!"

Eating with Children

A guy hosted a dinner party for people from work, including his boss. All during the sit-down dinner, the host's three-year-old daughter stared at her father's boss sitting across from her. The girl could hardly eat her food from staring.

The man checked his tie, felt his face for food, patted his hair in place, but nothing stopped her from staring at him. He tried his best to just ignore her, but finally it was too much for him.

He asked her, "Why are you staring at me?" Everyone at the table had noticed her behavior, and the table went quiet for her response.

The little girl replied, "My Daddy said you drink like a fish, and I don't want to miss it!"

Chapter 20. **You Must Be Joking** Work #4

The Smart Clerk!

A really huge, muscular guy with a bad stutter goes to a counter in a deptartment store and asks, "W-w-w-where's the m-m-m-men's dep-p-p-partment?" The clerk behind the counter just looks at him and says nothing.

The man repeats himself, "W-w-w-where's the m-m-m-men's dep-p-p-partment?" Again, the clerk doesn't answer him. The guy asks several more times, "W-w-w-where's the m-m-m-men's dep-p-p-partment?" And the clerk just seems to ignore him. Finally, the guy gets angry and storms off.

The customer who was waiting in line behind the guy asks the clerk, "Why wouldn't you answer that guy's question?"

The clerk answers, "D-d-d-do you th-th-th-think I w-w-w-want to get b-b-b-beat up?!!"

The local bar was so sure that its bartender was the strongest man around that they offered a standing $1,000 bet. The bartender would squeeze a lemon until all the juice ran into a glass and hand the lemon to a patron. Anyone who could squeeze one more drop of juice out would win the money. Many people had tried over time (weightlifters, longshoremen, etc.), but nobody could do it.

One day this scrawny little man came in, wearing thick glasses and a polyester suit, and said in a tiny, squeaky voice, "I'd like to try the bet." After the laughter had died down, the bartender said okay, grabbed a lemon, and squeezed away. He handed the wrinkled remains of the rind to the little man. But the crowd's laughter turned to total silence as the man clenched his fist around the lemon and six drops fell into the glass.

As the crowd cheered, the bartender paid the $1,000, and asked the little man, "What do you do for a living? Are you a lumberjack, a weightlifter, or what?"

The man replied, "I work for the IRS."

Chapter 20. **You Must Be Joking** Work #5

Lipstick

According to a news report, a certain private school in Victoria, BC was recently faced with a unique problem.

A number of grade 12 girls were beginning to use lipstick and would put it on in the bathroom. That was fine, but after they put on their lipstick, they would press their lips to the mirror, leaving dozens of little lip prints. Every night, the maintenance man would remove them, and the next day the girls would put them back.

Finally, the principal decided that something had to be done. She called all the girls to the bathroom and met them there with the maintenance man. She explained that all these lip prints were causing a major problem for the custodian, who had to clean the mirrors every night.

To demonstrate how difficult it had been to clean the mirrors, she asked the maintenance man to show the girls how much effort was required. He took out a long-handled squeegee, dipped it in the toilet, and cleaned the mirror with it.

Since then, there have been no lip prints on the mirror.

Promotion

The boss called one of his employees into the office. "Rob," he said, "you've been with the company for a year. You started off in the mail room, one week later you were promoted to a sales position, and one month after that you were promoted to district manager of the sales department. Just four short months later, you were promoted to vice-president. Now, it's time for me to retire, and I want you to take over the company. What do you say to that?"

"Thanks," said the employee.

"Thanks?" the boss replied "Is that all you can say?"

"I suppose not," the employee said. "Thanks, Dad."

Chapter 20. **You Must Be Joking**   Work #6

The Big Shake-up!

A company, feeling it was time for a shake-up, hires a new CEO. This new boss is determined to rid the company of all slackers. On a tour of the facilities, the CEO notices a guy leaning on a wall. The room is full of workers and he thinks this is his chance to show everyone he means business!

The CEO walks up the guy and asks, "And how much money do you make a week?" Undaunted, the young fellow looks at him and replies, "I make $200.00 a week. Why?" The CEO then hands the guy $200 in cash and screams, "Here's a week's pay, now GET OUT and don't come back!" Feeling pretty good about his first firing, the CEO looks around the room and asks, "Does anyone want to tell me what that slacker did here?"

With a sheepish grin, one of the other workers mutters, "Pizza delivery guy."

Stopping by the Office One Day

Wanting to surprise her husband, an executive's wife stopped by his office. She found him with his secretary sitting in his lap.

Without hesitating, he dictated, "...and in conclusion, gentlemen, shortage or no shortage, I cannot continue to operate this office with just one chair."

The Young Businessman

A young businessman had just started his own firm. He rented a beautiful office and had it furnished with antiques. Sitting there, he saw a woman come into the outer office. Wishing to appear the hot shot, the businessman picked up the phone and started to pretend he had a big deal working. He threw huge figures around and made giant commitments. Finally he hung up and asked the visitor, "Can I help you?"

The woman said, "Yeah, I've come to activate your phone lines."

Prepare Three Envelopes

A fellow had just been hired as the new CEO of a large high tech corporation. The CEO who was stepping down met with him privately and presented him with three numbered envelopes. "Open these if you run up against a problem you don't think you can solve," he said.

Well, things went along pretty smoothly, but six months later, sales took a downturn and he was really catching a lot of heat. About at his wit's end, he remembered the envelopes. He went to his drawer and took out the first envelope. The message read, "Blame your predecessor."

The new CEO called a press conference and tactfully laid the blame at the feet of the previous CEO. Satisfied with his comments, the press and Wall Street responded positively, sales began to pick up, and the problem was soon behind him.

About a year later, the company was again experiencing a slight dip in sales, combined with serious product problems. Having learned from his previous experience, the CEO quickly opened the second envelope. The message read, "Reorganize." This he did, and the company quickly rebounded.

After several consecutive profitable quarters, the company once again fell on difficult times. The CEO went to his office, closed the door, and opened the third envelope.

The message said, "Prepare three envelopes."

Chapter 20. **You Must Be Joking**   Politics #1

They say that Christopher Columbus was the first Democrat. When he left to discover America, he didn't know where he was going. When he got there he didn't know where he was. And it was all done on a government grant.

Q: What is a recent Democratic college graduate's usual question in his/her first job?

A: "Would you like fries with that?"

Difference Between Republicans and Democrats

A Republican and a Democrat were walking down the street when they came to a homeless person. The Republican gave the homeless person his business card and told him to come to his business for a job. He then took twenty dollars out of his pocket and gave it to the homeless person.

The Democrat was very impressed, and when they came to another homeless person, he decided to help. He walked over to the homeless person and gave him directions to the welfare office. He then reached into the Republican's pocket and gave the homeless person fifty dollars.

Now you understand the difference between Republicans and Democrats.

Ancient Republican Proverb:

Teach a man to light a fire and he will be warm forever. But throw him into the fire and he will never again complain about being cold.

Chapter 20. **You Must Be Joking** Politics #2

Rats

A tourist walks into a curio shop in San Francisco. Looking around at the exotica, he notices a very lifelike life-sized bronze statue of a rat. It has no price tag, but is so striking he decides he must have it. He takes it to the owner: "How much for the bronze rat?" "$12 for the rat, $100 for the story," says the owner. The tourist gives the man $12. "I'll just take the rat. You can keep the story." As he walks down the street carrying his bronze rat, he notices that a few real rats have crawled out of the alleys and sewers and begun following him down the street. This is disconcerting, and he begins walking faster. But within a couple of blocks, the herd of rats behind him has grown to hundreds, and they begin squealing. He begins to trot toward the bay, looking around to see that the rats now number in the MILLIONS, and are squealing and coming toward him faster and faster. Concerned, even scared, he runs to the edge of the bay and throws the bronze rat as far out into the water as he can. Amazingly, the millions of rats all jump into the bay after it and drown. The man walks back to the curio shop. "Ah ha," he says to the owner, "you have come back for the story?"

"No," says the man, "I came back to see if you have a bronze Republican."

A Liberal and a Genie

A liberal came upon a genie and said, "You're a genie. Can you grant me three wishes?" The genie replied, "Yes, but only if you're feeling generous enough to share your good fortune." The liberal said, "I'm a liberal. I'm always happy to share." The genie said, "O.K., then, whatever you wish for, I'll give every conservative in the country two of it. What's your first wish?" "I would like a new sports car." "O.K., you've got it, and every conservative in the country gets two sports cars. What's your second wish?" "I'd like a million dollars." "O.K., you get a million dollars, every conservative gets two million dollars. What's your third and final wish?"

"Well, I've always wanted to donate a kidney."

Chapter 20.   **You Must Be Joking**   Politics #3

AN AMERICAN CORPORATION: You have 2 cows. You sell one, and force the other to produce the milk of four cows. You are surprised when the cow drops dead.

A FRENCH CORPORATION: You have 2 cows. You go on strike because you want 3 cows.

A JAPANESE CORPORATION: You have 2 cows. You redesign them so they are one-tenth the size of an ordinary cow and produce twenty times the milk.

A GERMAN CORPORATION: You have 2 cows. You reengineer them so they live for 100 years, eat once a month, and milk themselves.

A BRITISH CORPORATION: You have 2 cows. They are mad. They die. Pass the shepherd's pie, please.

AN ITALIAN CORPORATION: You have 2 cows, but you don't know where they are. You break for lunch.

A RUSSIAN CORPORATION: You have 2 cows. You count them and learn you have 5 cows. You count them again and learn you have 42 cows. You count them again and learn you have 12 cows. You stop counting cows and open another bottle of vodka.

A SWISS CORPORATION: You have 5000 cows, none of which belong to you. You charge others for storing them.

AN INDIAN CORPORATION: You have 2 cows. You worship both of them.

A CHINESE CORPORATION: You have 2 cows. You have 300 people milking them. You claim full employment, high bovine productivity, and arrest the journalist who reported on them.

AN ARKANSAS CORPORATION: You have 2 cows. That one on the left is kinda cute.

Appendix

Time-O!   211
   A variation of ZINGO! for telling time

May I Ask Who's Calling Part 2   231
   Advanced skills in leaving & taking telephone messages

U.S. Currency   237
   Bills & coins

Phone Number Speed   245
   A variation of 1-2-3- Write! for giving & writing down phone numbers

Blank Game Chips   248
   An extra sheet of blank game chips to design your own custom games and/or activities

Time-O

Time-O! Study Sheet

twelve o'clock
noon (P.M.)
midnight (A.M.)

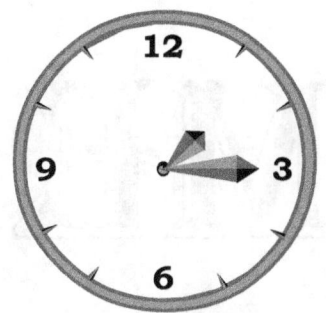

one fifteen
a quarter after one
a quarter past one

twelve thirty

half past twelve

one forty-five

a quarter to two

three o' five
five **after** three
five **past** three

one fifty

ten **to** two

one twenty-five

two forty

two o'clock

Time-O! Game Sheet #1

TIME-O!

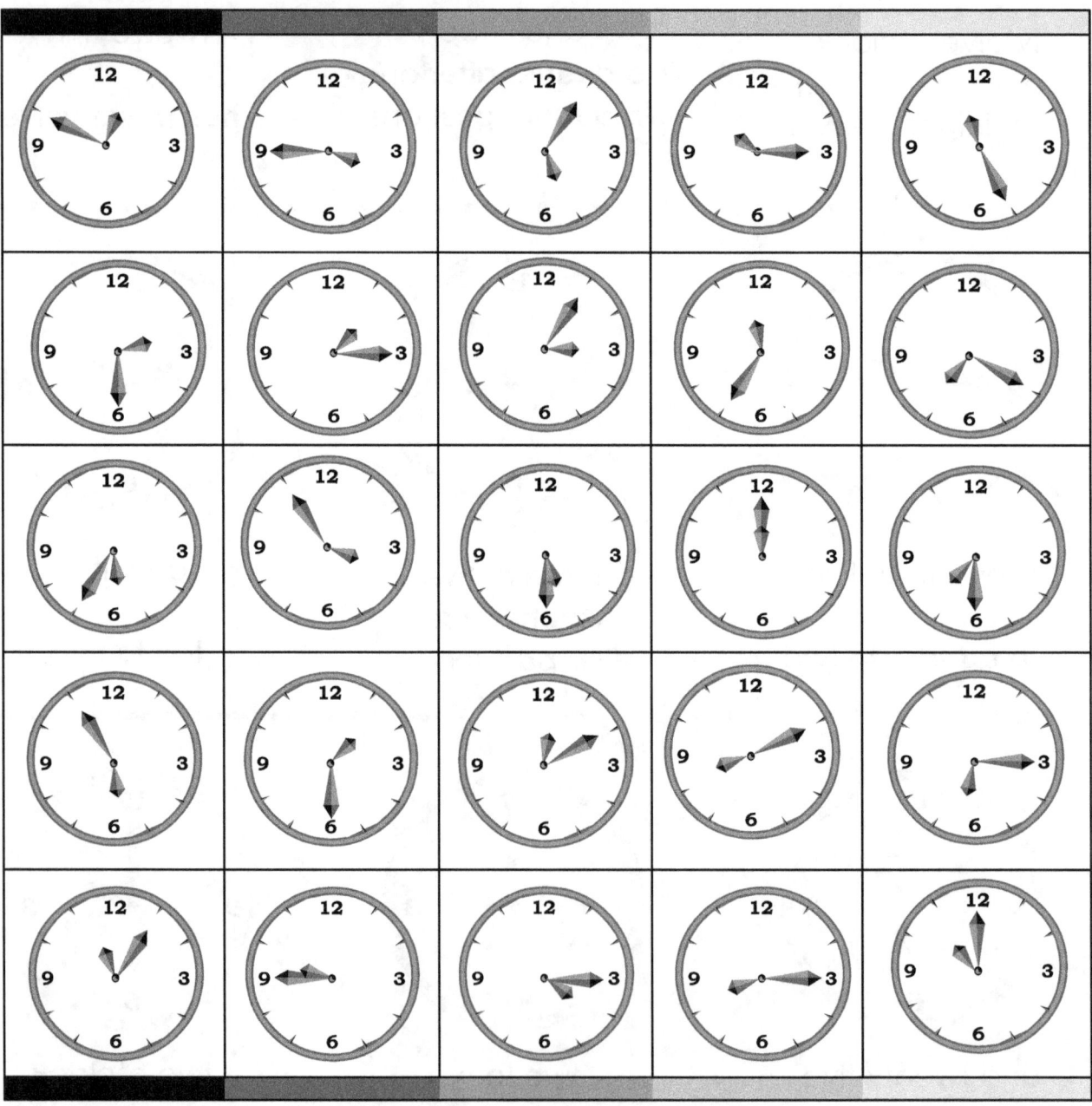

Page 212 **FUN, QUICK & EASY** - Game-Based Activities for Teachers of Adult ESL

Time-O! Game Sheet #2

TIME-O!

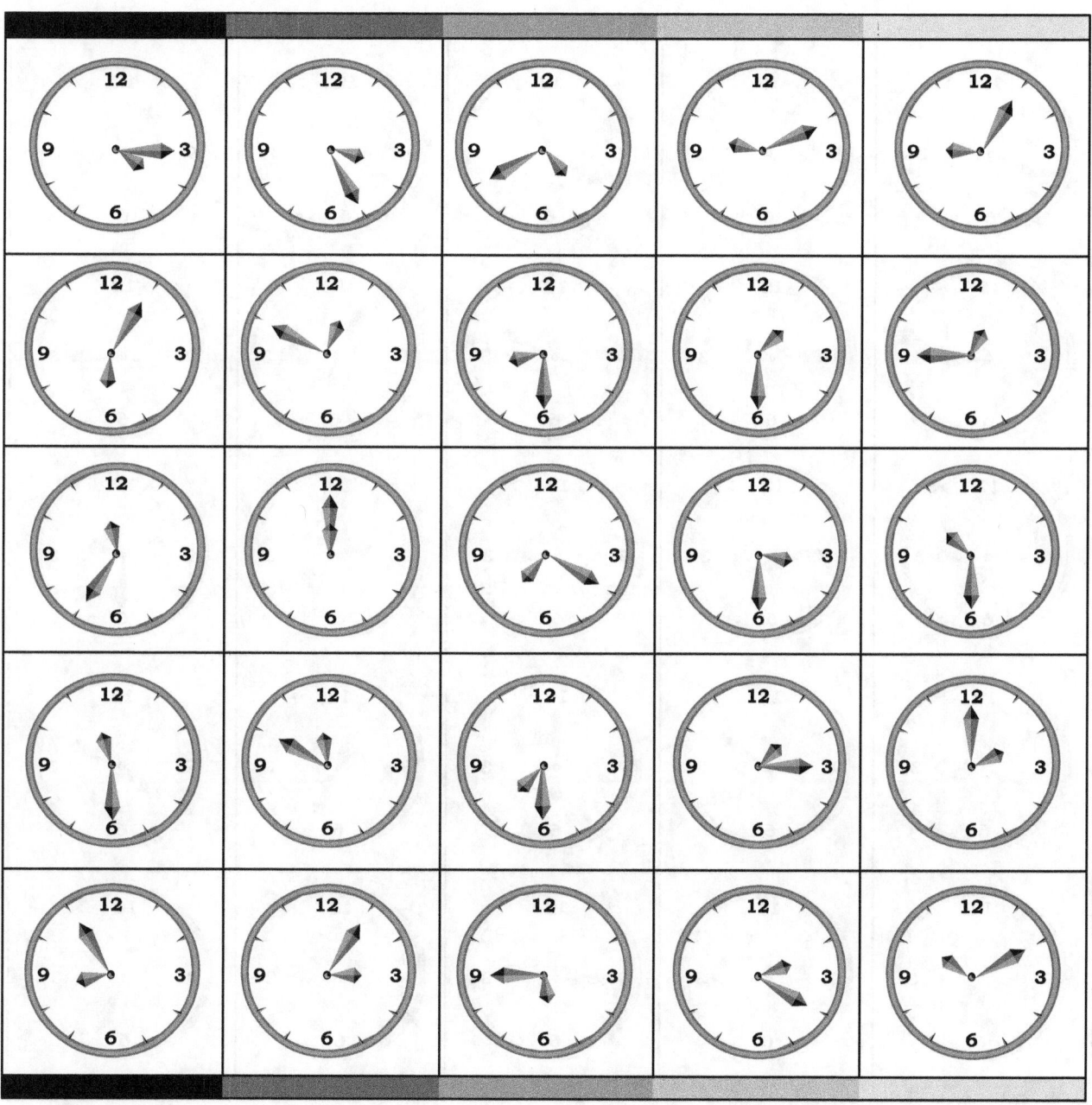

FUN, QUICK & EASY - Game-Based Activities for Teachers of Adult ESL

Time-O! Game Sheet #3

TIME-O!

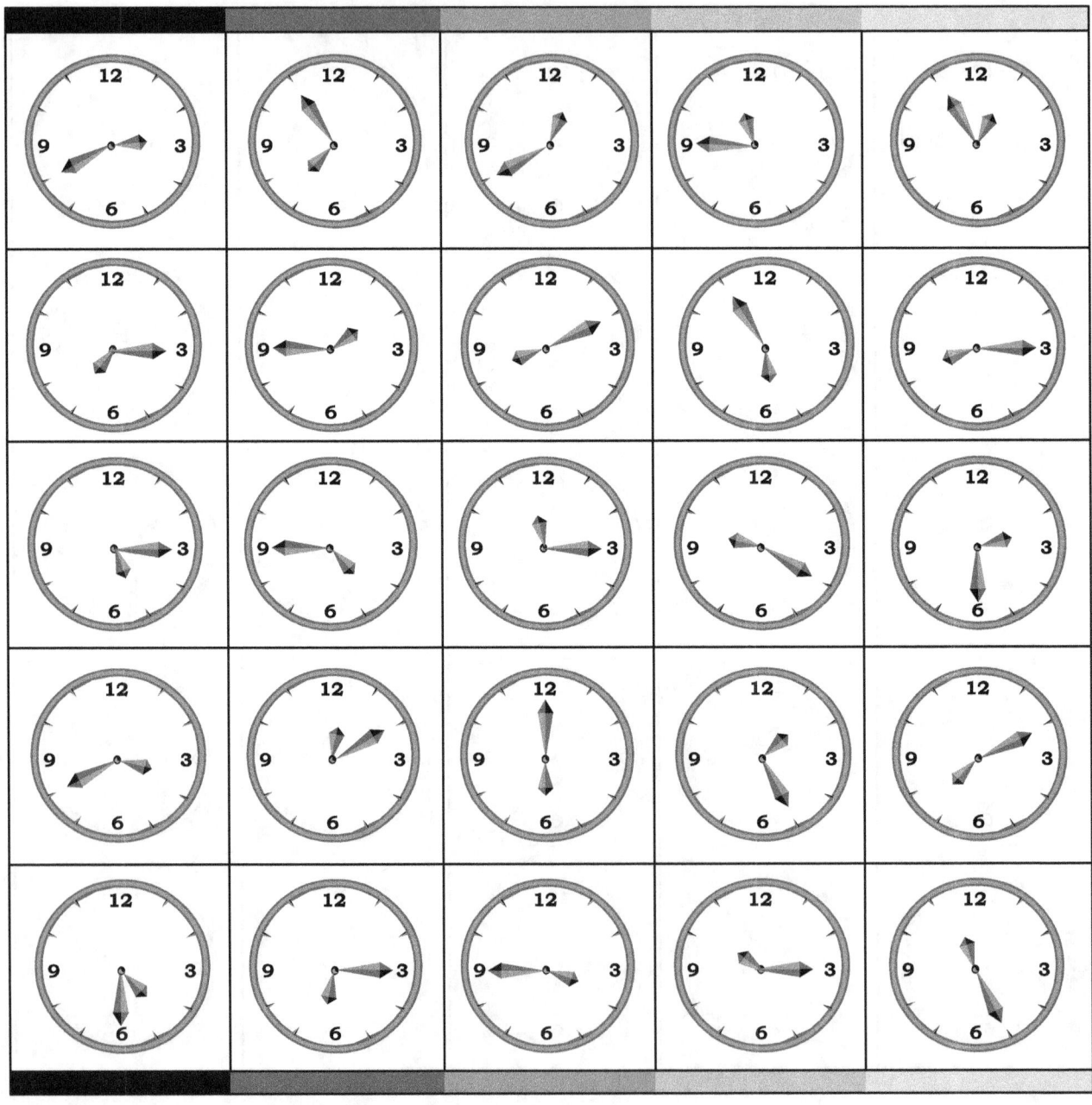

Page 214   **FUN, QUICK & EASY**   Game-Based Activities for Teachers of Adult ESL

TIME-O!

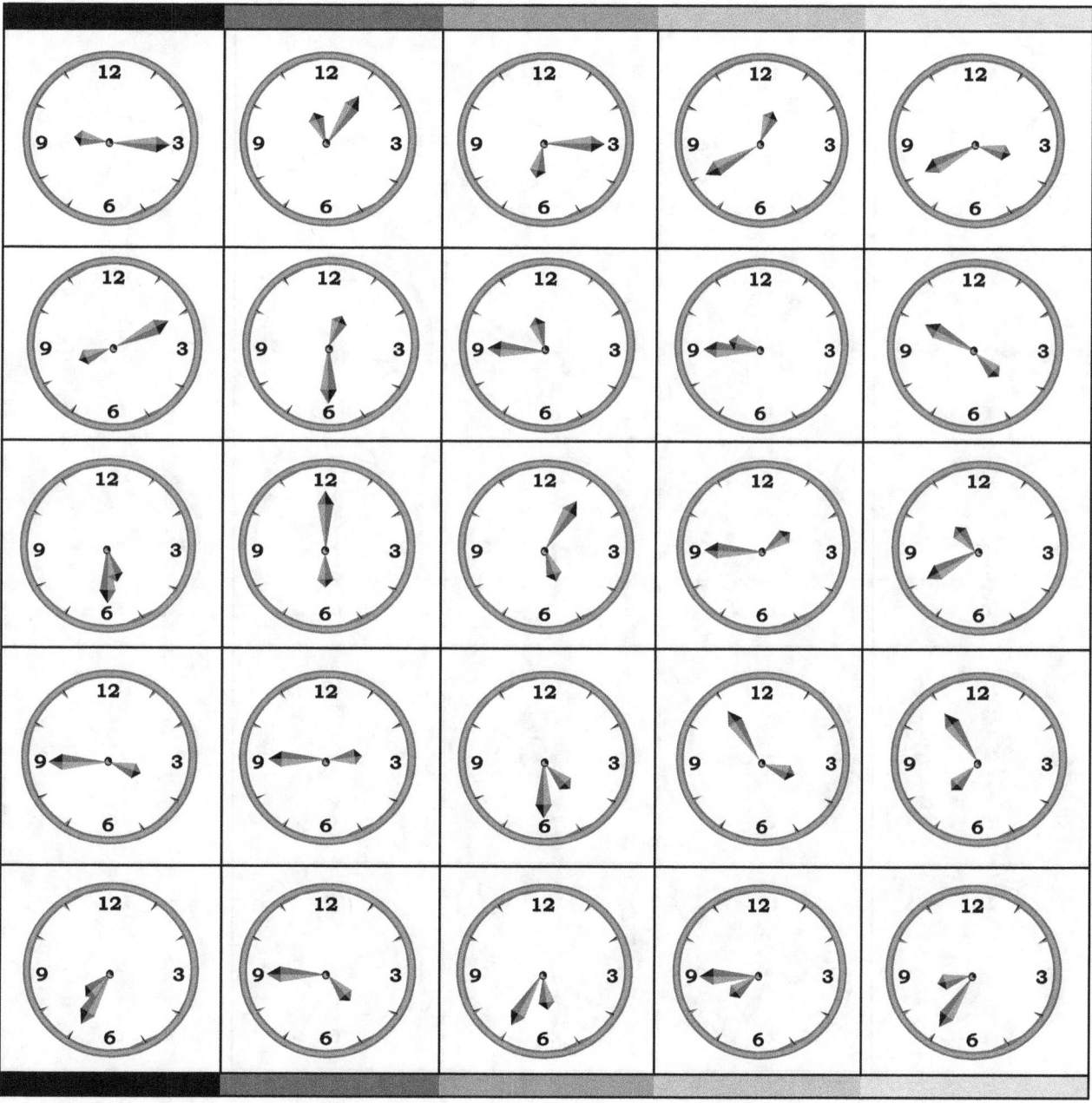

Time-O! Game Sheet #5

TIME-O!

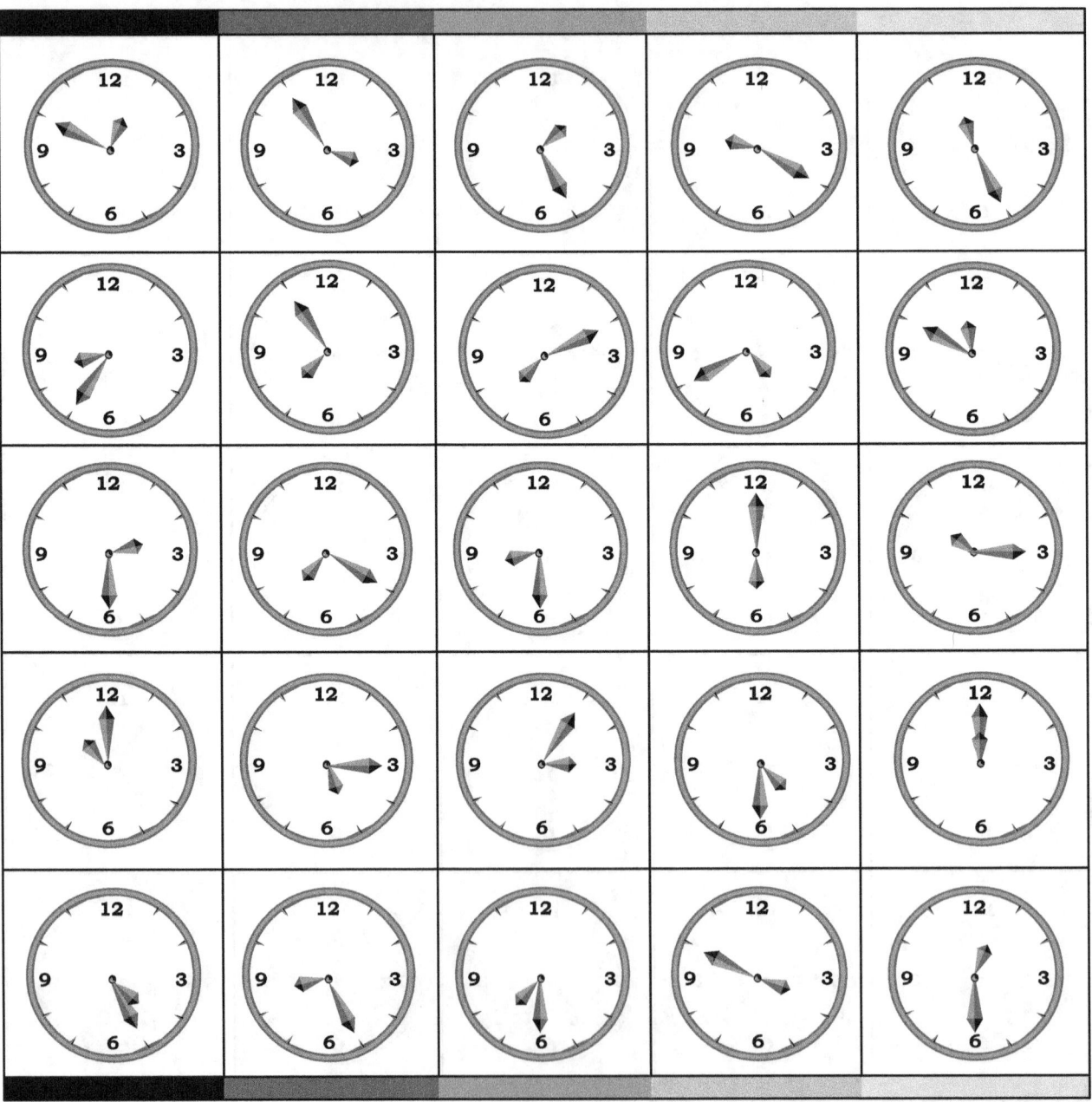

Time-O! Game Sheet #6

TIME-O!

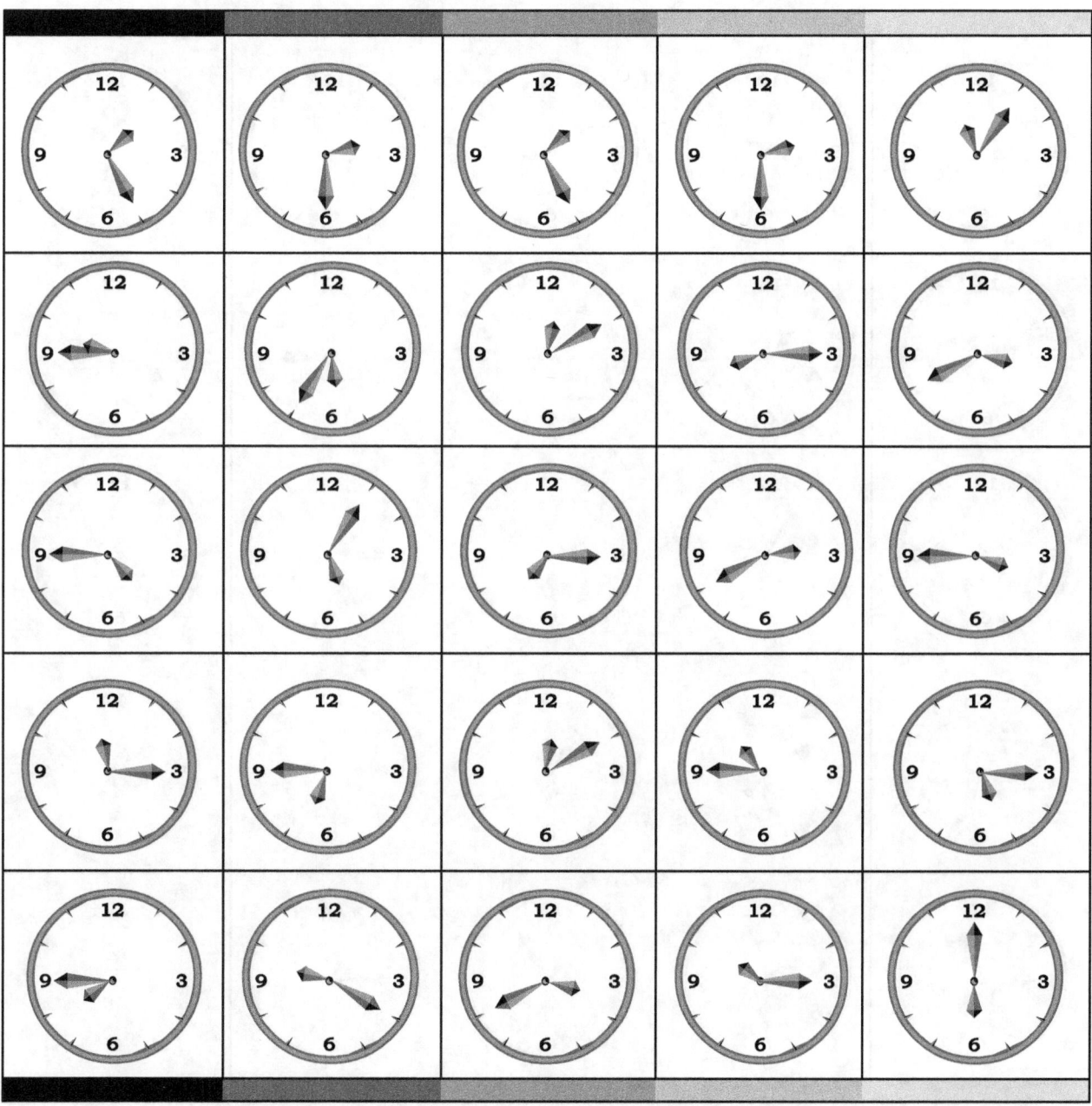

FUN, QUICK & EASY   Game-Based Activities for Teachers of Adult ESL

Time-O! Game Sheet #7

TIME-O!

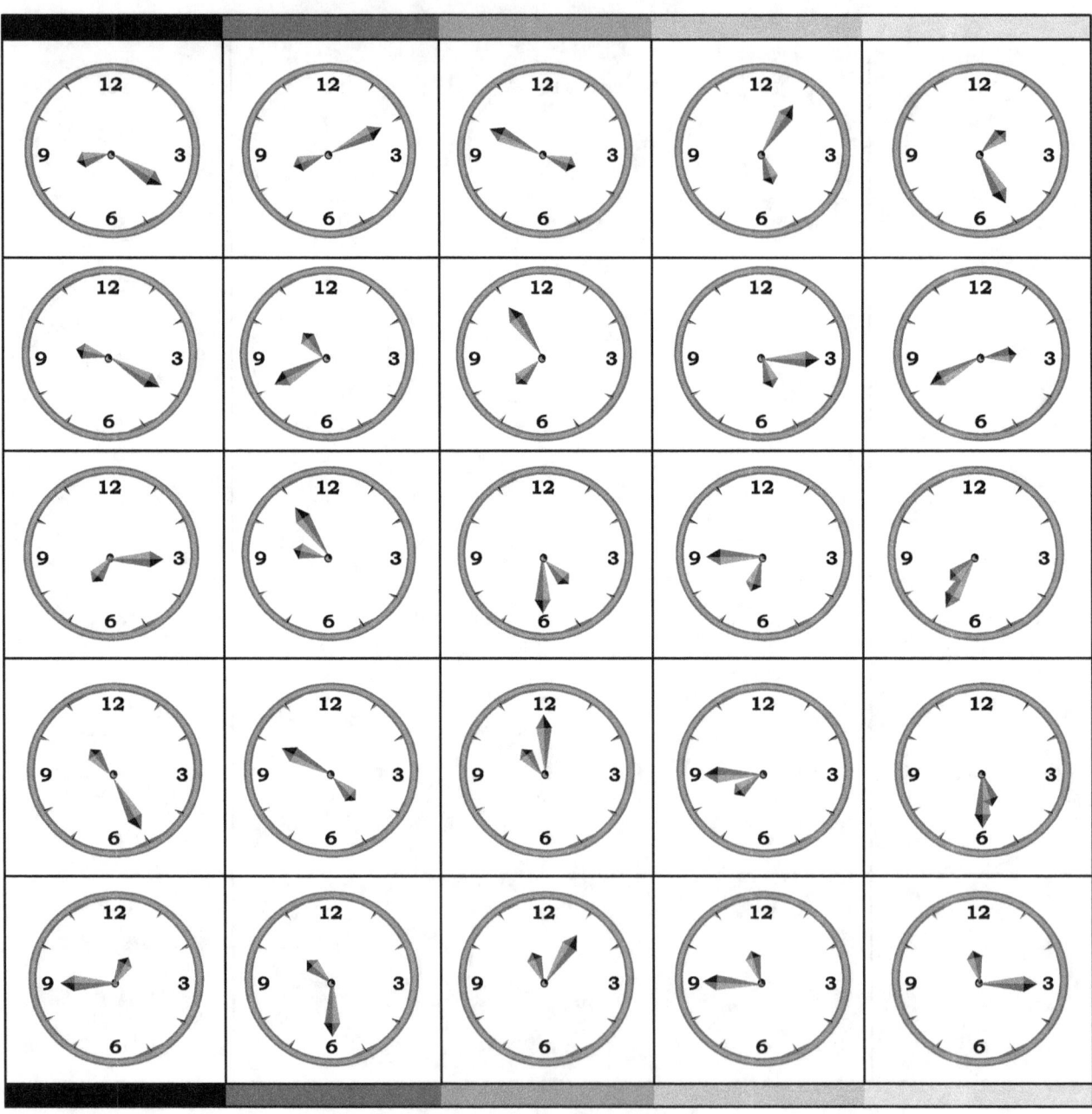

TIME-O!

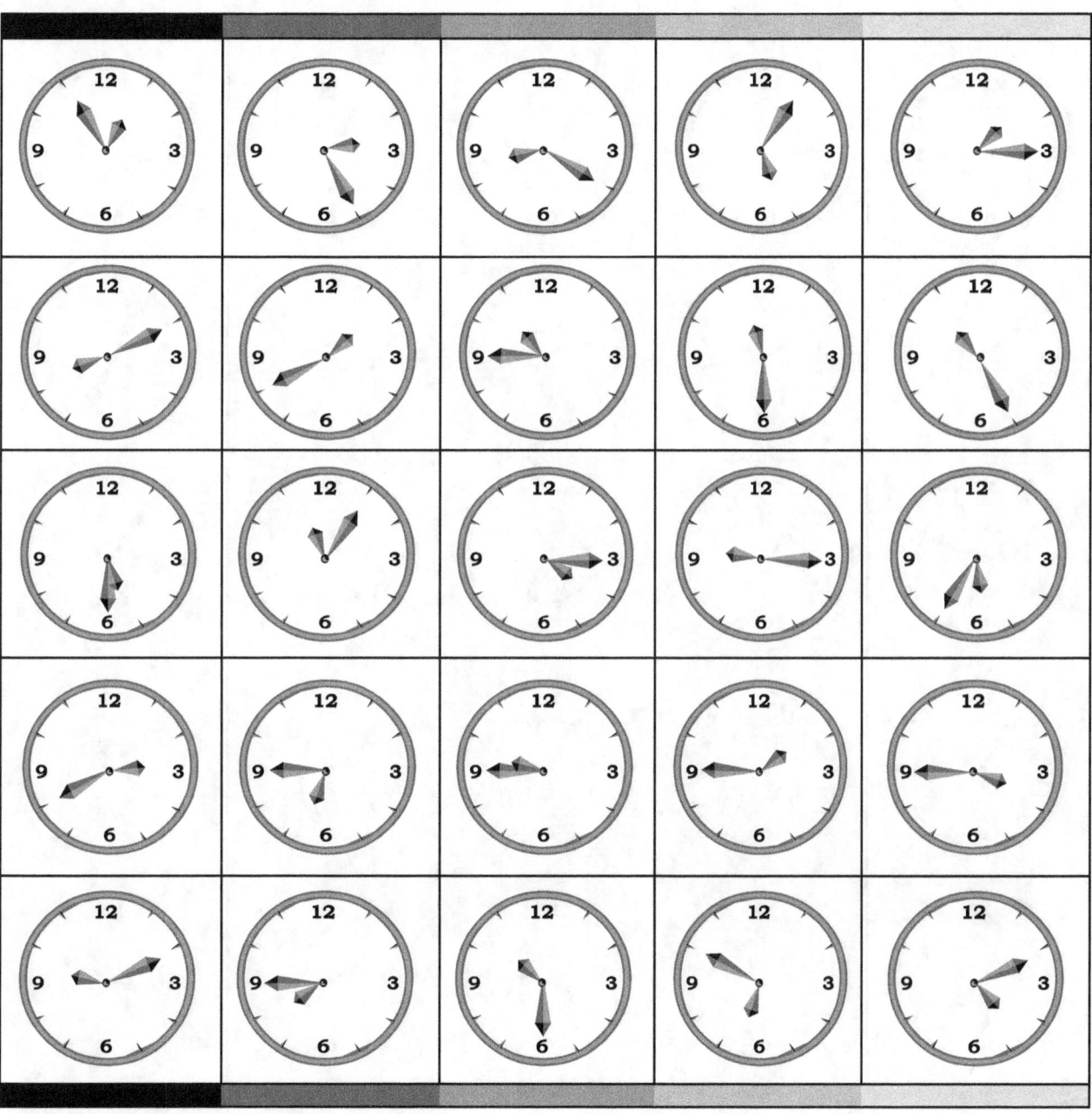

Time-O! Game Sheet #9

TIME-O!

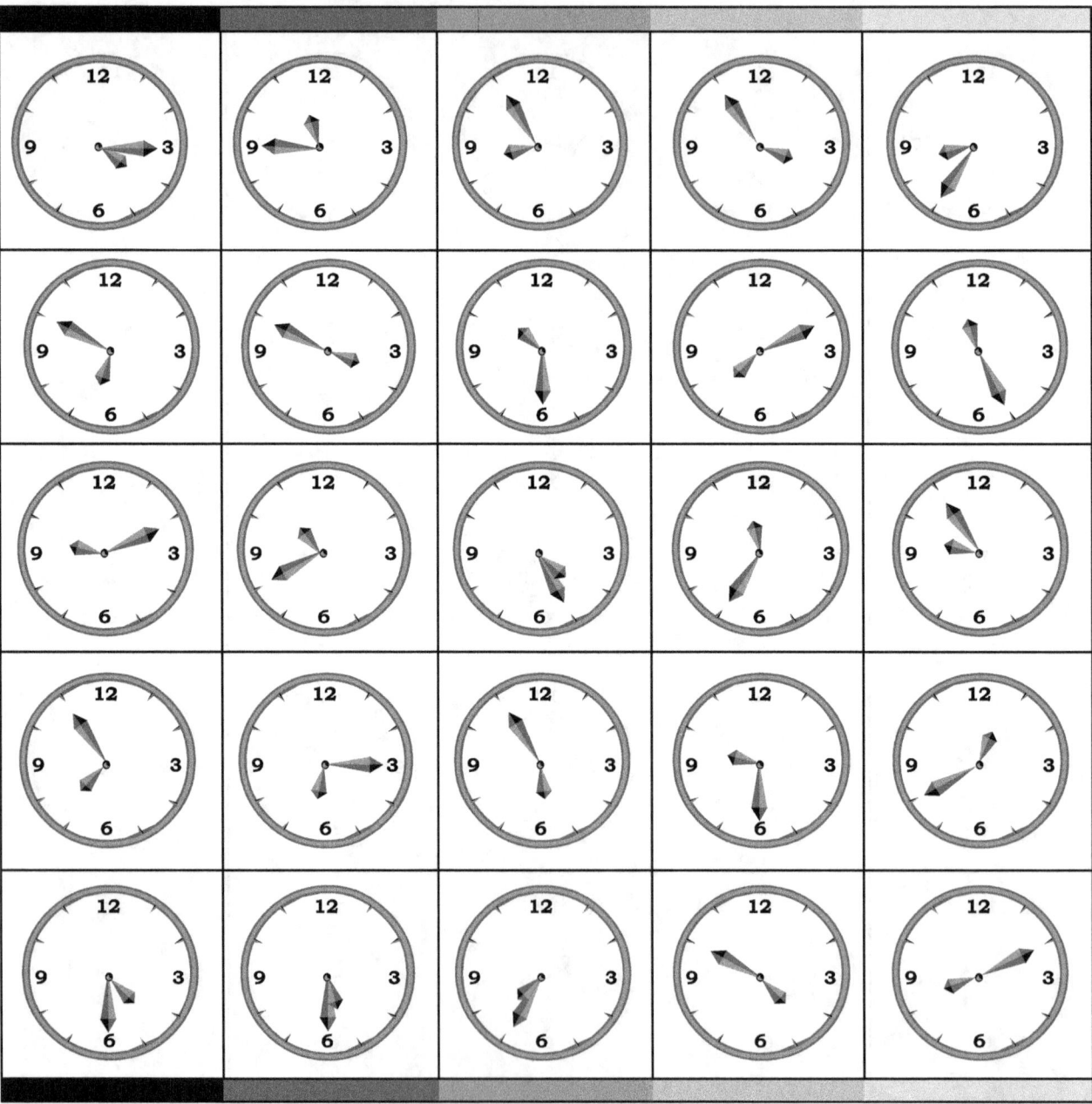

Page 220 FUN, QUICK & EASY Game-Based Activities for Teachers of Adult ESL

Time-O! Game Sheet #10

TIME-O!

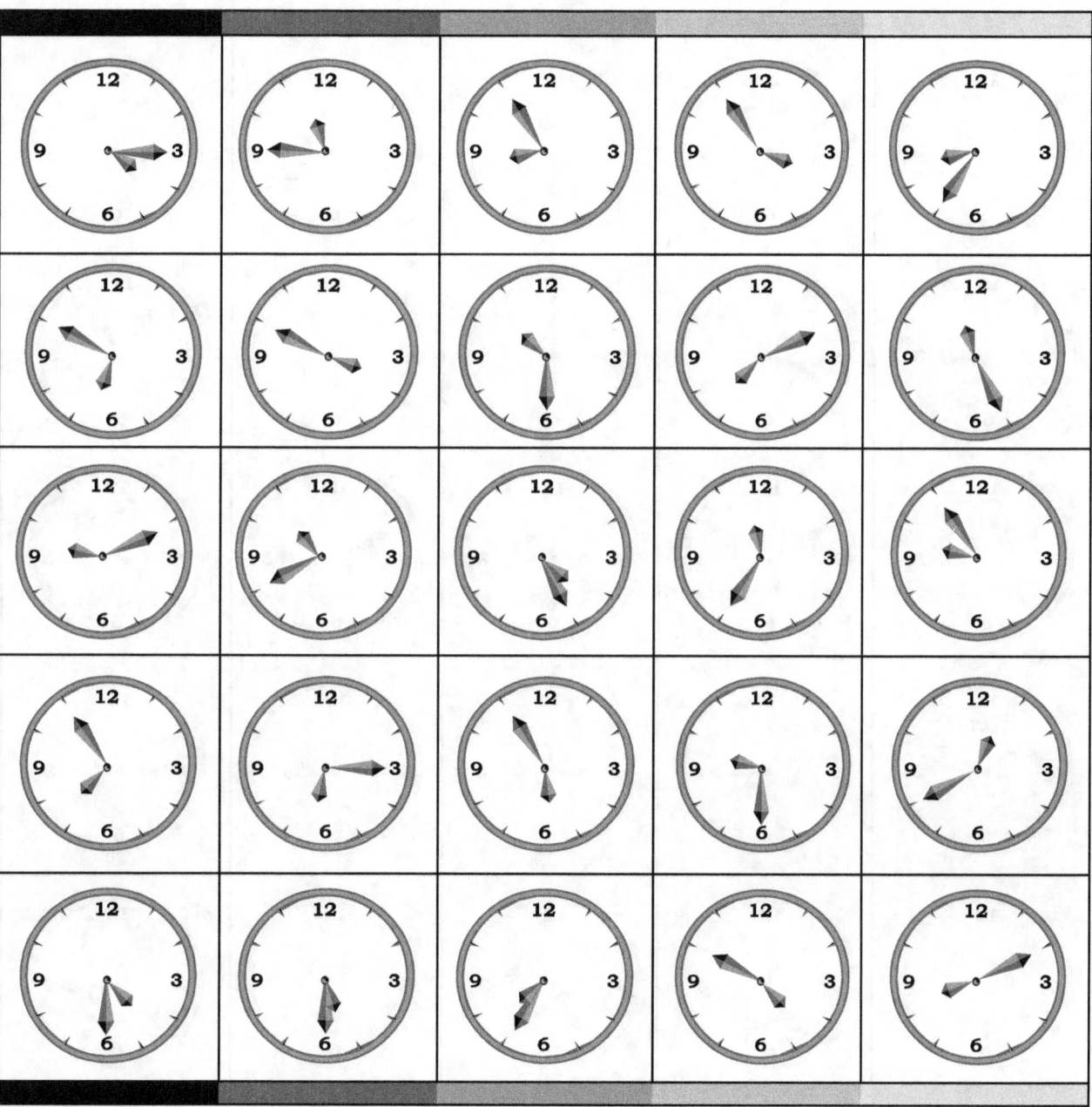

FUN, QUICK & EASY Game-Based Activities for Teachers of Adult ESL

Time-O! Game Sheet #11

TIME-O!

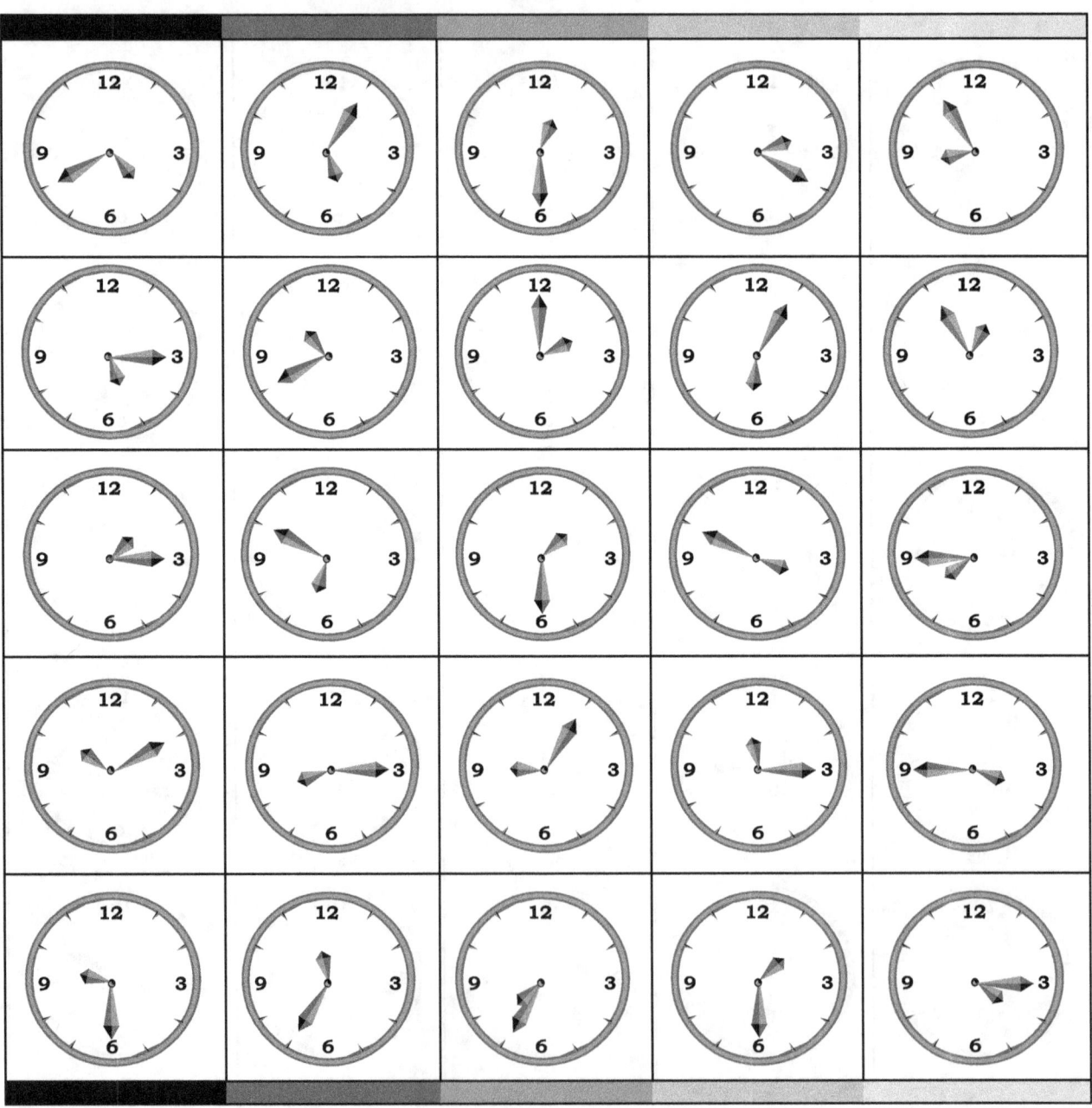

Page 222 — Fun, Quick & Easy — Game-Based Activities for Teachers of Adult ESL

Time-O! Game Sheet #12

TIME-O!

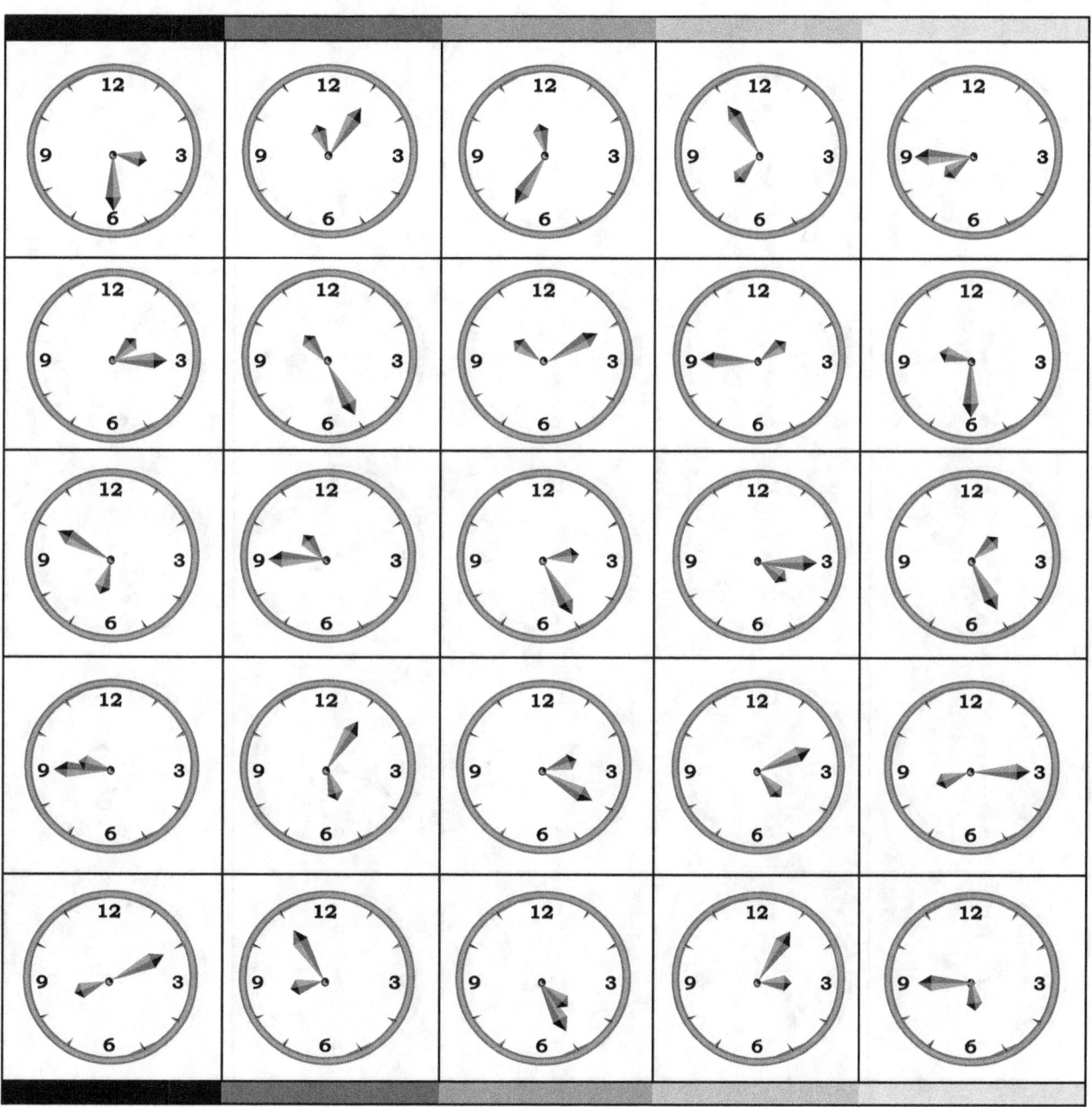

FUN, QUICK & EASY   Game-Based Activities for Teachers of Adult ESL

Time-O!   Game Sheet #13

TIME-O!

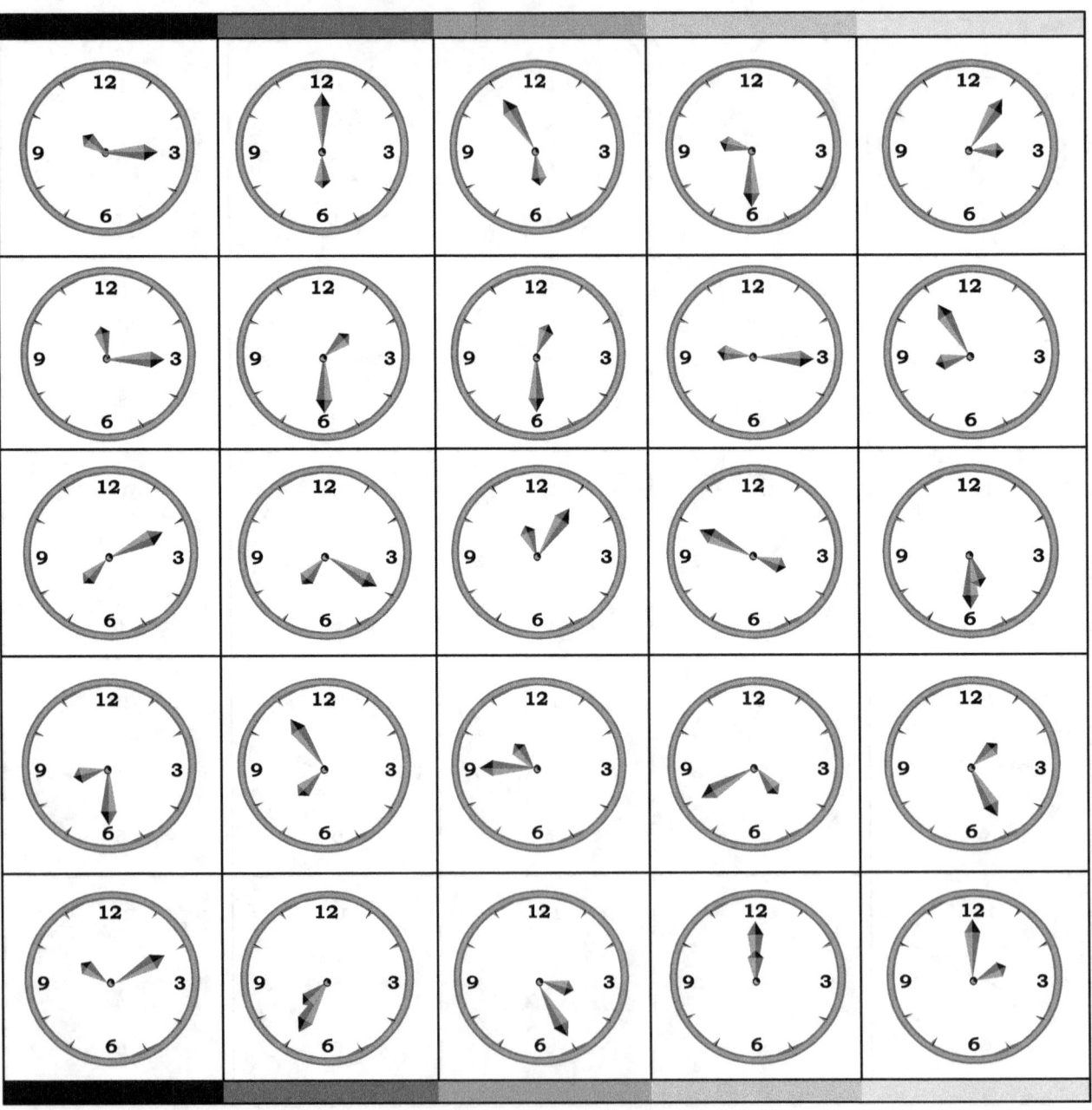

TIME-O!

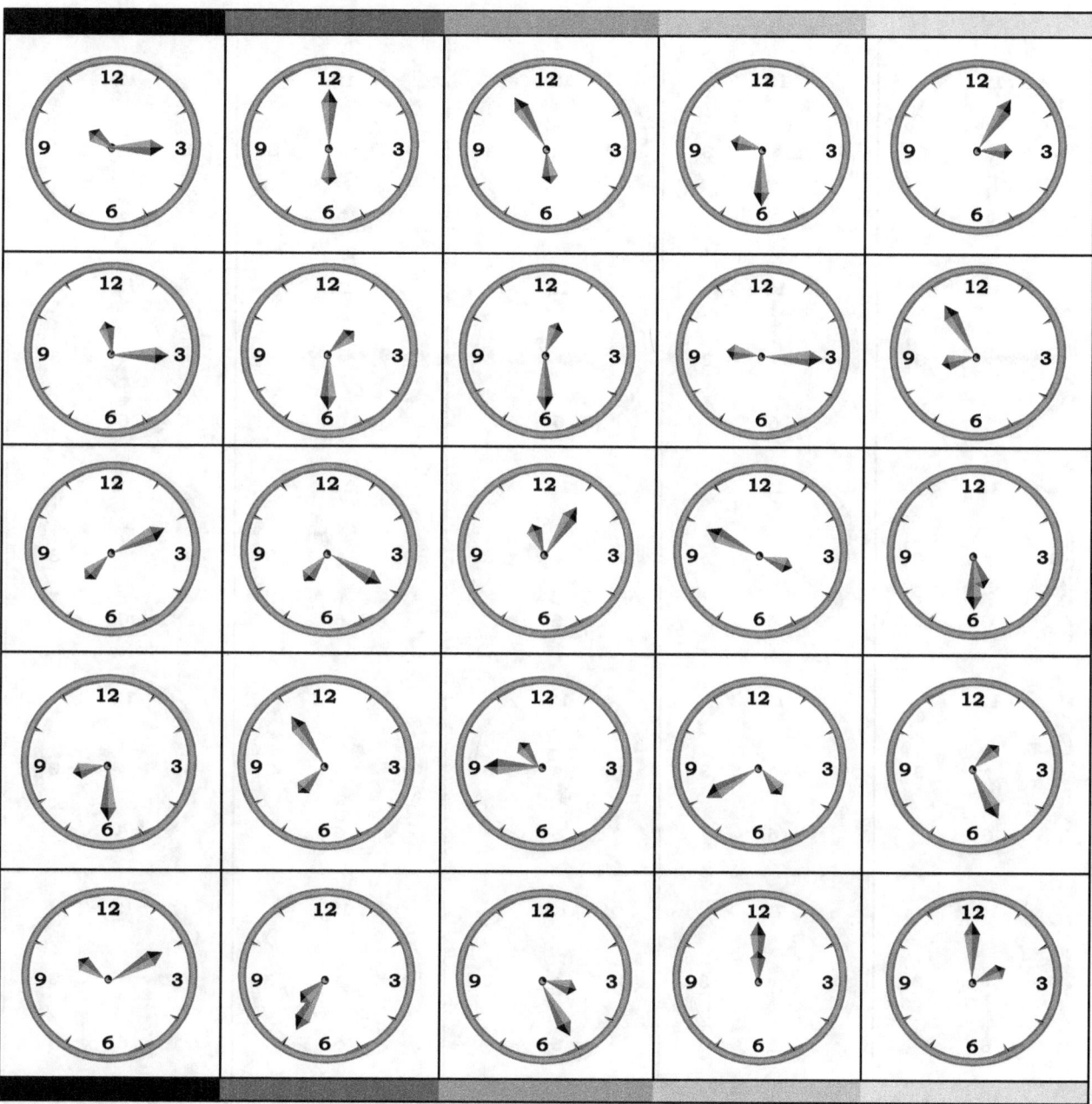

TIME-O!

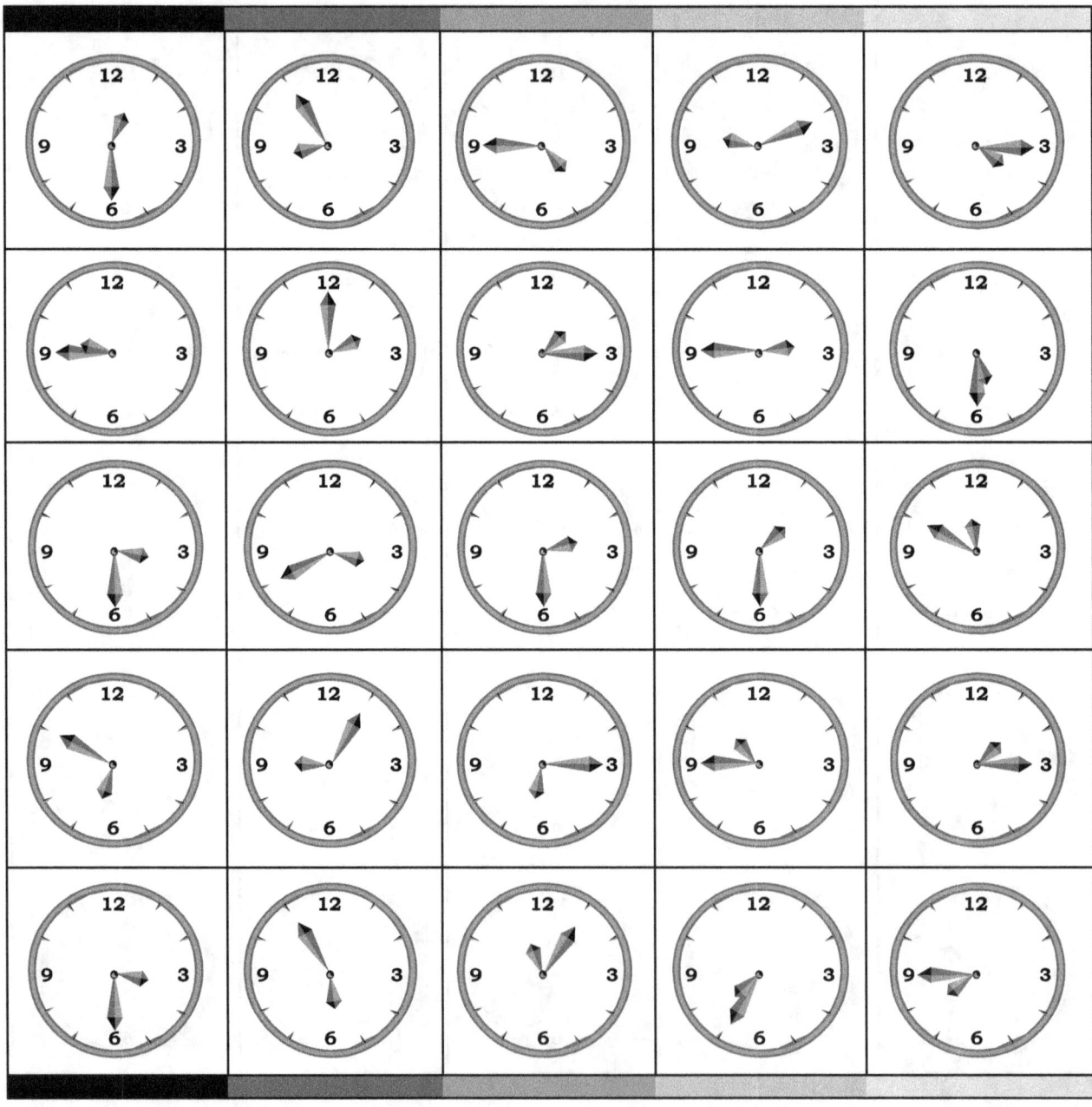

Appendix. **Time-O!** Game Chips #1

twelve o'clock noon midnight	twelve forty-five a quater **to** one	twelve ten ten **past** twelve ten **after** twelve	twelve fifty-five five **to** one	twelve thirty half **past** twelve
one fifteen a **quarter after** one a **quarter past** one	one thirty half **past** one	one twenty-five	one forty-five a **quarter to** two	one fifty ten **to** two
two o'clock	two twenty	two thirty half **past** two	two forty	two forty-five a **quarter to** three
three o' five five **after** three five **past** three	three thirty half **past** three	three forty	three forty-five a **quarter to** four	three fifty ten **to** four

Page 228 Appendix. **Time-O!** Game Chips #2

eight thirty **half past** eight	eight fifty-five **five to** nine	eight fifteen **a quarter past** eight **a quarter after** eight	eight twenty	eight thirty-five
nine o'five five **after** nine five **past** nine	nine ten ten **after** nine ten **past** nine	nine twenty	nine forty-five **a quarter to** ten	nine thirty **half past** nine
ten ten ten **after** ten ten **past** ten	ten thirty **half past** ten	ten fifteen **a quarter after** ten **a quarter past** ten	ten forty-five **a quarter to** eleven	ten forty
eleven fifty ten **to** twelve	eleven thirty-five	eleven fifteen **a quarter after** eleven **a quarter past** eleven	eleven o'five five **after** eleven five **past** eleven	eleven twenty-five

Appendix. **Time-O!** Game Chips #3

four forty	four fifteen **a quarter after** four **a quarter past** four	four forty-five **a quarter to** five	four ten ten **after** four ten **past** four	four thirty **half past** four
five forty-five **a quarter to** six	five thirty **half past** five	five fifteen **a quarter after** five **a quarter past** five	five o' five five **after** five five **past** five	five fifty-five five **to** six
six o'five five **after** six five **past** six	six fifty ten **to** seven	six o'clock	six forty-five **a quarter to** seven	six fifteen **a quarter after** six **a quarter past** six
seven twenty	seven thirty-five	seven fifteen **a quarter after** seven **a quarter past** seven	seven forty-five **a quarter to** eight	seven ten ten **after** seven ten **past** seven

Appendix. **Time-O!** Game Chips #4

twelve fifty ten **to** one	twelve forty	one forty	two twenty-five	three fifty-five five **to** four
three twenty-five	eight ten ten **after** eight ten **past** eight	eight twenty-five	nine fifteen **a quarter after** nine **a quarter past** nine	nine fifty-five five **to** ten
eleven thirty half **past** eleven	eleven forty-five **a quarter to** twelve	ten o'clock	ten twenty-five	four fifty ten **to** five
seven thirty **half past** seven	seven fifty-five five **to** eight	six twenty	five thirty-five	four twenty-five

Appendix. **May I Ask Who's Calling?** Phone Message Sheets

FOR _____ Urgent ☐	FOR _____ Urgent ☐
DATE _____ TIME _____ A.M. / P.M.	DATE _____ TIME _____ A.M. / P.M.
WHILE YOU WERE OUT	**WHILE YOU WERE OUT**
M _____	M _____
OF _____	OF _____
PHONE _____ AREA CODE NUMBER EXTENSION	PHONE _____ AREA CODE NUMBER EXTENSION
MESSAGE _____ _____ _____ _____	MESSAGE _____ _____ _____ _____
SIGNED	SIGNED
FOR _____ Urgent ☐	FOR _____ Urgent ☐
DATE _____ TIME _____ A.M. / P.M.	DATE _____ TIME _____ A.M. / P.M.
WHILE YOU WERE OUT	**WHILE YOU WERE OUT**
M _____	M _____
OF _____	OF _____
PHONE _____ AREA CODE NUMBER EXTENSION	PHONE _____ AREA CODE NUMBER EXTENSION
MESSAGE _____ _____ _____ _____	MESSAGE _____ _____ _____ _____
SIGNED	SIGNED

May I Ask Who's Calling? Part 2   Study Sheet

Ring! Ring!

Secretary: Crash Happy Computers. How may I help you?

Caller: I'd like to speak to Brian Richardson please.

Secretary: May I ask who's calling?

Caller: Certainly. This is Lucy Domingo from The Coffee Bean.

Secretary: I'm sorry. Mr. Richardson is in a meeting. Would you like to leave a message?

Caller: Yes. Please ask him to call me back. The computer we purchased from him doesn't seem to be working.

Secretary: I'll let him know right away. May I have your phone number please?

Caller: Yes, it's area code 467-241-0387.

Secretary: Okay I'll repeat that. You're Lucy Domingo from The Coffee Bean, your phone number is area code (467)241-0387, and you're having problems with your new computer.

Caller: Correct.

Secretary: I'll see that he gets your message, Ms. Domingo.

Caller: Thank you.

Secretary: You're welcome. Good bye.

Caller: Bye.

Appendix. **May I Ask Who's Calling? Part 2** Caller Game Cards

---

You are **John Anderson**.
You work for **H & M Computers**.
Your telephone number is **503-893-0192**.
You would like to speak to **Susan Hayes**.
If she is not in, leave a message.

Susan's shipment of computers has arrived. You would like Ms. Hayes to call you back to set a date for delivery and installation.

You are **Tina Washington**.
You work for **Interiors By Design**.
Your telephone number is **220-504-5783 ext 34**.
You would like to speak with **Thomas Fernandez**.
If he is not in, leave a message.

You would like Mr. Garcia to call you back to discuss what color carpeting he'd like for his office.

You are **Mike Bradley**.
You work for **Red Dragon Advertising**.
Your telephone number is **714-872-9673 ext 1034**.
You would like to speak to **Elizabeth Mills**.
If she is not in, leave a message.

You would like Ms. Mills to call you back to set up a time to meet and look over your promotional ads.

You are **Jennifer Montgomery**.
You work for **Prime Real Estate**.
Your telephone number is **802-519-0852 ext 450**.
You would like to speak with **Pierre Guimet**.
If he is not in, leave a message.

You would like Mr. Guimet to call you back. You have found someone interested in buying his house.

You are **William Kung**.
You work for **1st Choice Savings & Loan**.
Your telephone number is **953-028-1764 ext 88**.
You would like to speak to **Hillary Stevens**.
If she is not in, leave a message.

Ms. Stevens had called with some questions about her new checking account. You are returning her call. You would like her to call you back.

You are **Noriko Hashimoto**.
You work for **Big Brother Security**.
Your telephone number is **172-428-5377 ext 225**.
You would like to speak to **Jens Ullah**.
If he is not in, leave a message.

Mr. Ullah wanted to get a price quote on some security cameras and installation. You are returning his call.

You are **Edward Nelson**.
You work for **Howie Cheatum Law Firm**.
Your telephone number is **520-229-4871 ext 620**.
You would like to speak to **Victoria Lange**.
If she is not in, leave a message.

You have some legal documents that she needs to sign. You'd like her to call you back to set up an appointment.

You are **Maria Hernandez**.
You work for **20/20 Optical Solutions**.
Your telephone number is **744-397-8201**.
You would like to speak to **Tyrone Jackson**.
If he is not in, leave a message.

Mr. Jackson's new contact lenses are ready. He can pick them up anytime during business hours, Monday through Friday 9AM to 5 PM.

You are **Paul Robinson**.
You are the principal of **Green Leaf High School**.
Your telephone number is **321-654-9878 ext 75**.
You would like to speak to **Natalie Silverman**.
If she is not in, leave a message.

You would like Ms. Silverman to call you ASAP regarding her son.

You are **Linda Smith**.
You work for **Sweet Tooth Bakery**.
Your telephone number is **881-702-3361**.
You would like to speak to **Jack Fitzpatrick**.
If he is not in, leave a message.

The cake Mr. Fitzpatrick ordered is ready. He can pick it up anytime before 7PM.

You are **Lance Chance**.
You work for **Beehive Hair Salon**.
Your telephone number is **406-541-2233**.
You would like to speak to **Fiona Davenport**.
If she is not in, leave a message.

You had a last minute cancellation and can see Ms. Davenport this afternoon at 2PM. You would like her to call you back ASAP to confirm.

You are **Donna Simpson**.
You are the owner of **In A Snap Photography**.
Your telephone number is **603-501-3855 ext 225**.
You would like to speak to **John Reed**.
If he is not in, leave a message.

Mr. Romano's photographs are ready. He can pick them up anytime during business hours, Monday through Friday 9AM to 6 PM or Saturday from 12PM to 5 PM.

Appendix.   **May I Ask Who's Calling? Part 2**   Blank Game Cards   Page 235

I am _____.

I work for _____.

My telephone number is

(_____) _____ – _____ ext. _____.

I would like to speak to

_____ _____.

Your message. _____

_____

_____

I am _____.

I work for _____.

My telephone number is

(_____) _____ – _____ ext. _____.

I would like to speak to

_____ _____.

Your message. _____

_____

_____

I am _____.

I work for _____.

My telephone number is

(_____) _____ – _____ ext. _____.

I would like to speak to

_____ _____.

Your message. _____

_____

_____

I am _____.

I work for _____.

My telephone number is

(_____) _____ – _____ ext. _____.

I would like to speak to

_____ _____.

Your message. _____

_____

_____

Mr. / Ms. _____ is in a meeting.	Mr. / Ms. _____ is at lunch.	Mr. / Ms. _____ is on vacation.
Mr. / Ms. _____ is away from his/her desk.	Mr. / Ms. _____ is with a customer.	Mr. / Ms. _____ is with a client.
Mr. / Ms. _____ is on another line.	Mr. / Ms. _____ is not in yet.	Mr. / Ms. _____ is out for the day.
Mr. / Ms. _____ is in a meeting.	Mr. / Ms. _____ is at lunch.	Mr. / Ms. _____ is on vacation.
Mr. / Ms. _____ is away from his/her desk.	Mr. / Ms. _____ is with a customer.	Mr. / Ms. _____ is with a client.
Mr. / Ms. _____ is on another line.	Mr. / Ms. _____ is not in yet.	Mr. / Ms. _____ is out for the day.
Mr. / Ms. _____ is in a meeting.	Mr. / Ms. _____ is at lunch.	Mr. / Ms. _____ is on vacation.
Mr. / Ms. _____ is away from his/her desk.	Mr. / Ms. _____ is with a customer.	Mr. / Ms. _____ is with a client.
Mr. / Ms. _____ is in a meeting.	Mr. / Ms. _____ is at lunch.	Mr. / Ms. _____ is on vacation.

Appendix. **U.S. Currency** Page 237

Page 238   Appendix. **U.S. Currency**

$5 $5 $5 $5 $5

25 25 25 1 1 1 10 10 5 5

Appendix. **U.S. Currency**

THE UNITED STATES OF AMERICA — $10 TEN DOLLARS	25
	25
THE UNITED STATES OF AMERICA — $10 TEN DOLLARS	25
	1
THE UNITED STATES OF AMERICA — $10 TEN DOLLARS	1
	1
THE UNITED STATES OF AMERICA — $10 TEN DOLLARS	10
	10
THE UNITED STATES OF AMERICA — $10 TEN DOLLARS	5
	5

Page 240 Appendix. **U.S. Currency**

$20	25
$20	25
$20	25
	1
$20	1
	1
$20	10
	10
$20	5
	5

Appendix. **U.S. Currency**

- $50 bill
- $50 bill
- $50 bill
- $50 bill
- $50 bill

Coins: 25, 25, 25, 1, 1, 1, 10, 10, 5, 5

Page 242   Appendix. **U.S. Currency**

- $100 bill — 25
- $100 bill — 25
- $100 bill — 25
- — 1
- $100 bill — 1
- — 1
- $100 bill — 10
- — 10
- $100 bill — 5
- — 5

Appendix. **U.S. Currency**

THE UNITED STATES OF AMERICA — TWO $2 TWO — TWO DOLLARS	50
THE UNITED STATES OF AMERICA — TWO $2 TWO — TWO DOLLARS	50
THE UNITED STATES OF AMERICA — TWO $2 TWO — TWO DOLLARS	50
THE UNITED STATES OF AMERICA — ONE THOUSAND $1000 ONE THOUSAND — ONE THOUSAND DOLLARS	50
THE UNITED STATES OF AMERICA — ONE THOUSAND $1000 ONE THOUSAND — ONE THOUSAND DOLLARS	$1
	$1
	$1
	$1

Page 244   Appendix.   **U.S. Currency**

25	25	25	25	25
25	25	25	25	25
10	10	10	10	10
10	10	10	10	10
5	5	5	5	5
5	5	5	5	5
1	1	1	1	1
1	1	1	1	1
25	10	5	1	50
$1	$1	$1	50	50

Appendix. **Phone Number Speed** Game Chips Sheet #1

1(800)-255-8547	1(800)-853-6000	808-349-1198
503-165-9035	202-316-7952	605-487-1677
212-857-3369	719-374-8824	928-475-8644
541-824-7622	770-226-4187	619-756-3472
831-224-7548	939-548-5473	804-117-6452
514-365-2574	711-515-4184	732-554-7411
442-140-6047	559-468-1683	484-984-1149
318-245-7439	352-514-8248	281-654-8742
278-629-0674	409-521-7949	256-068-4945
253-684-1698	264-981-8401	305-442-1388

316-047-6804	380-584-0586	402-225-8060
311-687-9817	314-354-7854	330-040-8737
401-374-5454	339-871-6717	410-105-5005
418-354-9863	423-115-8117	412-565-4564
501-604-2457	508-804-9684	530-168-1553
515-685-3451	513-749-9632	540-365-9574
601-353-6781	626-875-3484	627-235-6056
617-354-1606	628-348-3050	689-314-2455
758-301-6048	707-315-7214	762-354-8124
701-354-0127	774-021-8944	785-354-5438

Appendix. **Phone Number Speed** Game Chips Sheet #3

809-718-1546	813-987-3505	828-684-0466
815-357-1654	844-301-9667	870-324-8462
906-117-2457	910-345-8874	925-557-3641
931-646-8211	936-637-9863	985-442-6848
211-354-7651	260-024-7853	284-762-5401
303-751-4628	310-771-4266	317-548-2268
408-187-0654	473-032-5614	441-241-7142
567-807-1244	530-648-0571	517-048-3547
651-804-0452	619-354-8965	689-772-5410
704-624-5472	718-345-9368	720-324-8465

Page 248　Appendix.　Blank Game Chips